28.70

Colorado Christian University
Library
180 S. Garrison
Lakewood, Colorado 80226

THE other AMERICA

Teen ALCOHOLICS

THE other AMERICA

Teen ALCOHOLICS

These and other titles are included in *The Other America* series:

Battered Women	Teen Addicts
Gangs	Teen Alcoholics
Gay and Lesbian Youth	Teen Dropouts
The Homeless	Teen Fathers
Homeless Teens	Teen Mothers
Illegal Immigrants	Teen Runaways
People with AIDS	Teens in Prison

THEotherAMERICA

Teen ALCOHOLICS

by
Gail B. Stewart

Lucent Books, P.O. Box 289011, San Diego, CA 92198-9011

Cover design: Carl Franzén

Library of Congress Cataloging-in-Publication Data

Stewart, Gail B., 1949–
    Teen alcoholics / by Gail B. Stewart.
        p. cm.—(The other America / Gail B. Stewart)
    Includes bibliographical references (p.   ) and index.
    Summary: Describes the lives of four teenage alcoholics, discussing
their problems, treatment, and ways in which they have dealt with their
addiction with varying degrees of success.
    ISBN 1-56006-606-7 (lib. bdg. : alk. paper)
    1. Teenagers—Alcohol use—United States Juvenile literature.
2. Alcoholics—United States Juvenile literature.   3. Alcoholism—United
States Juvenile literature. [1. Alcoholism.]   I.Title.   II. Series: Stewart,
Gail B., 1949–   Other America.
HV5135.S755   2000
362.292′0835′0973—dc21   96–35047
                                                                                                      CIP

The opinions of and stories told by the people in this book are entirely their
own. The author has presented their accounts in their own words, and has
not verified their accuracy. Thus, the author can make no claim as to the
objectivity of their accounts.

Printed in the U.S.A.
Copyright © 2000 by Lucent Books, Inc.
P.O. Box 289011, San Diego, CA 92198-9011

Contents

Foreword

O, YES,
I SAY IT PLAIN,
AMERICA NEVER WAS AMERICA TO ME.
AND YET I SWEAR THIS OATH—
AMERICA WILL BE!
LANGSTON HUGHES

Perhaps more than any other nation in the world, the United States represents an ideal to many people. The ideal of equality—of opportunity, of legal rights, of protection against discrimination and oppression. To a certain extent, this image has proven accurate. But beneath this ideal lies a less idealistic fact—many segments of our society do not feel included in this vision of America.

They are the outsiders—the homeless, the elderly, people with AIDS, teenage mothers, gang members, prisoners, and countless others. When politicians and the media discuss society's ills, the members of these groups are defined as what's wrong with America; they are the people who need fixing, who need help, or increasingly, who need to take more responsibility. And as these people become society's fix-it problem, they lose all identity as individuals and become part of an anonymous group. In the media and in our minds these groups are identified by condition—a disease, crime, morality, poverty. Their condition becomes their identity, and once this occurs, in the eyes of society, they lose their humanity.

The Other America series reveals the members of these groups as individuals. Through in-depth interviews, each person tells his or her unique story. At times these stories are painful, revealing individuals who are struggling to maintain their integrity, their humanity, their lives, in the face of fear, loss, and economic and spiritual hardship. At other times, their tales are exasperating,

8

demonstrating a litany of poor choices, shortsighted thinking, and self-gratification. Nevertheless, their identities remain distinct, their personalities diverse.

As we listen to the people of *The Other America* series describe their experiences they cease to be stereotypically defined and become tangible, individual. In the process, we may begin to understand more profoundly and think more critically about society's problems. When politicians debate, for example, whether the homeless problem is due to a poor economy or lack of initiative, it will help to read the words of the homeless. Perhaps then we can see the issue more clearly. The family who finds itself temporarily homeless because it has always been one paycheck from poverty is not the same as the mother of six who has been chronically chemically dependent. These people's circumstances are not all of one kind, and perhaps we, after all, are not so very different from them. Before we can act to solve the problems of the Other America, we must be willing to look down their path, to see their faces. And perhaps in doing so, we may find a piece of ourselves as well.

Introduction

Kari is a sixteen-year-old who seemed, until recently, to have everything going for her. She is an honor student and a member of her school's swim team. She is well liked. Her family is loving and supportive.

ANOTHER KARI

But Kari had another side that no one else saw. This Kari suffered from blackouts—times when she seemed awake but was unaware of what she was doing. When she experienced blackouts, she did things that she would not normally do.

"I've done things like slap people, get right in their faces," Kari admits. "I don't usually swear, but I've had times when I've blacked out and totally came apart—I called this one girl every horrible word I could think of. Friends told me the next day and I didn't believe them!"

This Kari had times when she felt that no one really understood her. She experienced depression and anxiety. She carried a bottle of vodka in her purse—even to school. She drank when no one was around—in the bathroom at school, in her room at home. She stole liquor from her parents' cabinet and replaced what she stole with water so that the bottles appeared untouched.

Kari told herself that she could stop drinking at any time, but she was not sure of that, not really. She was aware that her grades were slipping, and her parents were concerned about her health. She explained her hangovers as a touch of the flu or as fatigue.

Last October Kari was arrested for driving drunk, and she tearfully confronted her parents and told them she had a drinking problem. "I felt like I had hit bottom," she says. "My parents were so bewildered. They were like, 'But Kari, we didn't know you even drank.' That's how good I was at fooling everyone. Including myself."

Kari is getting treatment for her condition, but she knows that she will always be an alcoholic. "Even if I never touch another drop, I know that I have the potential to abuse alcohol," she says. "Other people can drink and not experience the same behavior, the same cravings. But I'm not like other people."

A GROWING PROBLEM

Kari is one of a growing number of teenage alcoholics in the United States—a number that is climbing at an alarming rate. Four percent of American teens say they drink daily, and half of those teens admit to being drunk almost every day. Approximately 250,000 teens enter alcohol abuse treatment programs each year, and many experts say that for every teen who is receiving treatment, several more should be but are not. In fact, the National Institute on Alcohol Abuse and Alcoholism (NIAAA) estimates that between 5.2 and 5.5 million teenagers are alcohol abusers.

The majority of teen alcoholics say they began drinking before the age of ten.

This is surprising, especially considering that until recently most experts simply believed that teens could not become alcoholics. "Of course, we knew that there were plenty of young people who used alcohol," says Sadie Barnes, a treatment counselor from Chicago. "We knew kids drank too much, we knew they sustained alcohol-related injuries such as those resulting from automobile accidents or fights. But the symptoms we associated with alcoholism—brain damage, liver damage, things like that—we thought they were many years removed from that sort of thing."

In the past several years, however, doctors and treatment centers have found that their earlier thinking was flawed. While most teen drinkers have not drunk long enough to develop the easily distinguished symptoms of alcoholism, many of them have developed a strong addiction to alcohol and cannot stop drinking without help.

"To say that adolescents can't be addicted to alcohol is as wrong as an earlier stereotype—that women can't be alcoholics," says one treatment worker. "There are supposedly well-informed people who still believe that alcoholics are old skid row bums, and that's it. Well, that isn't the case. The truck drivers, the surgeons, the ministers, the mothers and fathers, and the kids—all of them can be alcoholics."

STARTING EARLIER

The younger a child starts drinking, say doctors, the greater the risk of becoming dependent on alcohol. Since a child's nervous system is not yet fully developed, the effects of alcohol—even a small amount—are more intense. Alcohol is absorbed faster into young people's bloodstreams; they will become drunk on less alcohol than an adult and will stay drunk longer.

How young are teen alcoholics when they start drinking? These statistics are grim: About 67 percent of thirteen-year-olds have used alcohol. Almost 88 percent of teen alcoholics say that they began drinking before they were ten years old, and some were as young as eight. Two out of every five children have drunk a wine cooler by the time they are thirteen.

"I was drinking beer after Little League games," remembers one nineteen-year-old alcoholic. "My dad kept it in the refrigerator in the basement, only he'd hardly ever use it—not unless there was a party. So my friend and I would go down there in the summer and chug a beer when we were hot after a baseball game. We were eight or nine—and we'd stumble around, feeling really buzzed."

Anthony, another teen alcoholic, began drinking heavily at age nine. "My parents would let me have sips of their drinks at parties back when I was four or five," he says. "And I got to like the taste, especially gin and tonics. By the time I was in third or fourth grade, I was stealing alcohol from the liquor cabinet or from other kids' houses at parties."

FAR-RANGING EFFECTS

Teens who abuse alcohol may suffer serious physical effects; however, the emotional and social effects can be just as devastating. For instance, adolescents who drink heavily are more likely to have difficulty in school, both academically and socially. Good students stop doing homework assignments and studying for tests—or they stop attending school on a regular basis.

"I spent most of eighth grade and half of ninth grade skipping school," says Marguerite, sixteen. "I used to be a good student—I was usually on the honor roll. But when I started using [alcohol] on a daily basis, school seemed like the most unimportant thing I could be doing with my time."

Ray, seventeen, says that his peer group changed when he began drinking. "I was starting on the varsity soccer team for my school as a freshman," he says. "And I used to hang out with those guys. But over the summer, between ninth grade and tenth grade, I started hanging with different kids. And it was easier to just stop going to soccer practice and go drink at my friend's house after school. I wish now that I hadn't done that—I got kicked off the team. I'll never know how good I could have been, and I won't get that chance again."

Teen alcoholics make more irresponsible choices than their sober counterparts, too. They are more likely to drink and drive; in fact, alcohol-related accidents are the number-one cause of death for young people between the ages of fifteen and twenty-four. Teens who drink heavily are more likely to engage in unprotected sex, too. A 1994 study found that 60 percent of teenage girls who have been diagnosed with a sexually transmitted disease say they were drunk at the time they were infected.

Alcohol addiction is also dangerous because it frequently leads to other drug use. For this reason, it is called a "gateway" drug.

Many alcoholics use marijuana, for example, to ease the unpleasant effects of a hangover. It is more and more common, say treatment workers, to find teens who are addicted to both drugs and alcohol.

WHY START?

Adolescents start using alcohol for many reasons. Drinking is considered a form of rebellion against parents and teachers. "I did it because I thought it would shock my parents," says one teen. "It was completely different from what they thought I was—a good little girl who never would do anything wrong. I thought that by drinking I was showing them that I wasn't a kid anymore."

Many teens begin using alcohol because they enjoy being drunk. It offers instant gratification; and, if a teen is bored, drinking is considered an interesting diversion. Experts say that is one of the differences between teens who drink and adults who drink: While many adults enjoy the camaraderie of drinking with others or the taste of the alcohol, teens who abuse alcohol do it solely to get drunk. "I didn't do it for the taste—are you kidding?" asserts one teen. "I hated it. I don't think I ever liked the smell of it at all, either. It was just a means to an end. The quicker I could be drunk, the better off I was."

One common reason why teens abuse alcohol is because being drunk provides an escape. Many teens find their lives are stressful or difficult. They may feel pressure from parents, teachers, or coaches—or even from themselves—to succeed. They may be shy or feel awkward around their peers and realize that "getting a buzz" provides a means of loosening up.

One teen felt embarrassed because she was overweight. As a result, she avoided social situations where she might feel uncomfortable. She began drinking heavily in high school and found some solace there. "The bottle was my friend," she says simply. "It was the only one I had."

A TOUGH ROAD

As with adult alcoholics, a teen alcoholic almost never seeks help right away when drinking becomes a problem. Common among many alcoholics is the denial that they even have a problem. It takes a crisis, often called "bottoming out" by counselors, to make the alcoholic realize that he or she needs help. Matt, seventeen,

The effects of alcohol are many, including accidents where alcohol has impaired the driver's judgment.

was involved in an accident when he was driving drunk. Although no one was killed, a woman was hospitalized with broken bones because of Matt's reckless behavior. "I was charged with a crime," he says. "But the worst part wasn't that—it was realizing all of a sudden what had become of me. I didn't think I was that bad. Friends tried to tell me not to drive, but I wouldn't listen. All of a sudden, I had to listen."

Some teens find help in treatment facilities or clinics. These places provide counseling in a controlled setting and allow teens to sort out the reasons why they began abusing alcohol. This treatment often includes attendance at Alcoholics Anonymous (AA), an organization that frequently hosts groups just for teens.

When the teen is ready to resume "normal" life, it is important to decide what aspects of his or her old life need changing and what can remain the same. "To just send a young alcoholic back to the same neighborhood, the same family, the same friends, without some sort of plan, that's a recipe for failure," says one counselor. "Often it's the peer group that helped the teen start his drinking life in the first place. Sure, you can't change where the young person lives, or who his family is. But it's important for him to be aware of the kinds of behaviors he needs to avoid the next time."

Tina, fifteen, knew she had to be more vocal about the kinds of stress she felt from her family, which was one of the reasons she drank. A combination of family counseling and consistent attendance at AA meetings have helped her. "My life isn't perfect," she says. "I know every day is a challenge. But there are some parts of my life that I can work on, things I can try to control. For me to stay sober, those things are a must."

FOUR DIFFERENT STORIES

In *The Other America: Teen Alcoholics,* four teen alcoholics tell very different stories. Ezra, sixteen, was addicted to marijuana before he started drinking heavily. Before being in treatment, he was expelled and suspended from a number of schools. He now attends Sobriety High, a small high school in Minnesota for teens who have had substance abuse problems. He feels more comfortable in this setting, he says, because people understand the kinds of problems he has had.

Melissa is an outgoing nineteen-year-old who was able to successfully hide her alcoholism from her mother. She drank, she says, to relieve the "bad messages" her brain sent to her—feelings that she was not attractive, outgoing, or smart enough. She has found help in her involvement with AA, both as a participant and as a sponsor of other young alcoholics.

Joe, eighteen, drank and used drugs out of boredom. "All the kids in my little town drank and got high," he says. "That's all there was to do." He has been to treatment numerous times, in numerous settings, although he is not sure whether it has helped him yet. At the time of his interview, he had been kicked out of his halfway house for using alcohol.

Miranda, sixteen, is another student at Sobriety High. Outgoing and social since she was very young, Miranda says she got in with a bad group of kids in junior high when she began having problems getting along with her mother. A chronic runaway, Miranda says she was as addicted to that behavior as she was to alcohol. She attends AA meetings as part of her school requirement, but she is uncertain whether she will continue with meetings when she is older.

All four are dealing with their alcoholism in different ways, with various degrees of success.

Ezra

"WE'D DO A GROUP SESSION EACH DAY, AND I'D HAVE CLASSES THERE, TOO. AND NO, IF YOU'RE GOING TO ASK IF IT HELPED ME, IT DIDN'T. I'D COME HOME FROM THE TREATMENT CENTER EACH DAY AND I'D KEEP HANGING OUT WITH MY FRIENDS, SELLING WEED, SMOKING IT, AND DRINKING. I DIDN'T CARE AT ALL; I DIDN'T WANT HELP."

Author's Note: Sixteen-year-old Ezra began his substance abuse with marijuana and later moved on to alcohol. He considers himself addicted to both, and he attends weekly support meetings. Ezra is a student at Sobriety High, an alternative high school for teens with substance abuse histories. He is very defensive of his family, with whom he has regained a closeness since treatment. Ezra seems a good example of a teen who can be a nightmare for teachers and principals—and parents—but who, with the right treatment, can drastically turn himself around.

The scene outside Sobriety High is not unlike that of any other school. A few yellow buses idle in front, their drivers nodding to one another. A middle-aged blond woman in a Jeep Cherokee chats on a car phone while keeping an eye out for her daughter, whom she is picking up for an early dentist appointment.

Inside the building, however, it is like no other high school. The entire student body—forty-five students—is gathered in a circle in the main room. The students are taking turns voicing concerns about fellow students who seem troubled or angry. One girl speaks up, telling the group that Tracy seemed unhappy and distracted, and she wanted to remind her that they are all supporting her. A boy with a long blond ponytail praises one of the younger boys, who stayed after school the day before to play Ping-Pong. "Way to go, Justin," the others sing out. "Nice going."

After a few final words the teens are dismissed, and Ezra walks over. He is a sixteen-year-old boy of mixed race with a strong deep voice that seems almost too big for his still-small frame. He walks into a conference room and sits on the sofa.

"Some people might be offended to be labeled an alcoholic," he begins. "But it doesn't bother me—not unless you're saying it to disrespect me or to make fun of me. I mean, to say I'm an alcoholic is like saying I live in a white house or that I'm wearing a blue shirt. It's the truth. It's who I am—who I have been for two or three years."

"Really a Happy Childhood"

Ezra comes from a large family; he and his five siblings and their parents live in an attractive house in the city. The neighborhood is one in which tall oaks and maples line the street.

"There's six kids in our family," he says. "I've got two younger siblings and three older. The four oldest of us are adopted; Isaac and Elizabeth are my parents' biological children. We all get along fine. My mom is a social worker at a hospital and my dad is a bishop. He's sort of the overseer of all the Lutheran churches in the city.

"I have had trouble the past several years in my life," Ezra says honestly. "I don't need anyone to explain that to me—I'm aware of it. And I've caused a lot of pain in my family, but that's not always how it's been. I mean, mine was really a happy childhood.

"There were always kids to play with, and our family does a lot together. We have a cabin, and we spend a lot of time there. At home I grew up doing stuff like everyone else, I guess. I played sports through the park teams and just had fun. I played soccer, baseball, hockey. I still play hockey just for fun, but I'm not on any team or anything now."

Troubles at School

Ezra says that he was a pretty normal kid until fourth grade. It was then that he began experiencing some difficulties in the school he attended.

"I got diagnosed as having attention deficit hyperactive disorder—ADHD," he says. "I was having a lot of trouble concentrating. I'd be like fidgety, wanting to move around. I couldn't sit still and do my work; I'd get distracted really easy.

"I got put on medication for it, and maybe it helped a little. But I still had trouble. That's kind of when things started going wrong. It wasn't all because of being ADHD; that didn't cause me to be an alcoholic," he insists. "But I got into some bad behavior stuff because of it.

"Like, I'd get up and the teachers would tell me to sit down. Sometimes I'd do it, but other times I'd just get mad. I'd yell or walk out of the room and slam the door. I'd get detentions for that, yeah. But it didn't seem to make that much difference because I'd just do it again the next time.

"As I got into fifth grade, and then into sixth, things were getting worse. I was getting in fights with other kids, I'd swear at

Ezra describes his childhood as happy and continues to play his favorite sports such as hockey.

teachers, just sort of fly off the handle. It's just like I really didn't care if they gave me detentions or anything. They'd call my parents, and they'd be mad, but I didn't care. The minute I got in trouble at school or got scolded for anything, I'd just get mad. It was like a pattern that I wasn't getting out of."

INTRODUCTION TO MARIJUANA

It was at this point in his life that Ezra was introduced to marijuana. He had tried beer once or twice—sneaking it with friends—but it was "weed" that really appealed to him at first.

"It's kind of ironic, I guess," he says. "I've probably had more trouble with alcohol in my life—I was drinking a little bit when I was ten or eleven—but as far as serious using, I started with weed. For a lot of kids with alcohol problems, it's the other way around. But in my life, the weed came first. And I was into it pretty heavy.

"I knew that kids were smoking it, of course. I mean, you hear things, you know? But none of my close friends were yet. But I went to visit this one friend of mine up north a ways. He used to live near me, but his family moved. Anyway, when I was there, he asked me if I'd smoked weed before, and I told him no. He asked me if I wanted to try it, and I said sure. I mean, I wasn't shocked or anything.

"We smoked it in the closet in his room," Ezra remembers. "I didn't really get high or anything. I liked the smell, I remember that. But as far as getting high or whatever, no. So it wasn't like I was really in a hurry to do it again soon."

However, not long after that Ezra found some marijuana in his own house.

"It was in my older brother's stuff," he says quietly. "I was doing a lot of stealing back then—taking money from my brothers and sisters and my mom, too. I'd buy CDs, clothes, stuff like that. It wasn't that hard to do. All my brothers and sisters had cash in their rooms; and my mom always had her purse somewhere around.

"I was really selfish back then," he continues. "I mean, I was just sort of acting like I was entitled to money, and so I'd take it. I don't do that anymore. But anyway, that's how I found the stuff in my brother's room. He had a little bit in a little safelike thing on his dresser. So I took it and went down to the creek near our house and smoked it.

"That time I really got high. I liked it a lot. I called my friend—the one I'd smoked with before—and told him I'd done it again and it was cool. It was a kind of nice feeling; I just watched some TV and went to sleep, I think. Anyway, it wasn't long after that that I found some kids in my neighborhood that were using it and selling it, too. So I had a supply that I could get myself."

"I JUST WANTED THE POWER"

At first Ezra was able to compartmentalize his drug use; he would smoke a little on weekends once in a while. He never called attention to his marijuana use, so his family was unaware that he was using it.

"I was twelve," he says. "And I spent a lot of time with my friends or outside. I started selling it, too. It was an easy way to get money, so I could buy more. It seemed like a good system at the time. There was one time in sixth grade, during the summer, that I got caught. I was at a church camp, and someone smelled the weed on me, I guess. They searched my suitcase and found it, and I got sent home. My mom and dad were mad, sure, but they didn't know the extent of it—how much I was using and that I was selling it.

"There were more problems at home, though. It was during sixth grade—I was twelve—that I bought a pellet gun from some kid in my neighborhood who went to a different school, Anthony. I stuffed the gun in my pants, or whatever, and brought it home. I just had it under my bed. Anyway, it turned out that kids were talking about it at Anthony—just cross talked, you know—and the liaison person at Anthony called someone at my school.

"They called me down and asked me about it," Ezra remembers. "But I lied; I denied knowing anything about it, and they didn't say anything more about it. I guess they called my dad at work, too, but I didn't know that. Anyhow, I went home after school and went down to the creek, smoked a little weed. And my dad came home like a half hour after I did, and when I got back, he started yelling at me. He was yelling real loud, asking me why I would get a gun. I told him I didn't even have it, and I got mad.

"I was sitting on my bed, and I reached underneath and pulled the gun out. It wasn't even loaded, but I pointed it at him. I just wanted the power, I guess—power over him so he couldn't yell at me. He ran out of the house; he didn't know it was just a pellet gun, so he was afraid. It looked like a real gun. He went next door and called the police, and they came and got me. I was taken to a mental health unit of the hospital, and I was there one night. My dad came and got me the next day, and that was that."

Changing Schools

"School was a problem, too," says Ezra. "After sixth grade my problems at school were so bad that my school suggested that I change. The school really wanted me to leave. It wasn't one particular thing that forced it, just a whole lot of me not cooperating. The school said it wasn't a good fit, their program and me. I wasn't doing well, and I had so many suspensions I wasn't getting anything out of it. My parents agreed, so I went to kind of an alternative program at a school called Northeast Junior High. The deal there was I'd stay in one room for the whole day. I'd get a lot more individualized attention and that would help me learn better.

"I didn't like Northeast at all," he says frowning. "I didn't think it helped me learn any better. I wasn't really hanging out with kids from there, either. I mean, I always had a lot of friends; I just make friends easily. And I had some people I got along with at Northeast, but my closest friends were all people from my neighborhood who were going to this one school called Anthony."

Expelled

Ezra says that his use of alcohol and drugs was increasing as a seventh grader.

"I'd go to Northeast for school during the day, but as soon as I got home I'd go up to Anthony and hang out after school with those guys. We'd smoke weed together on the weekends and sometimes during the week. We'd drink, too, and just kind of hang out.

"I was selling drugs at school, too, and I got in trouble for that. I sold it to this one kid, and he got caught. He told them I'd sold it to him, and so I got in trouble. That was bad enough, I guess, but it happened a second time. And the same thing—he got caught and told them where he'd gotten the weed, and so I got expelled. I had to leave the school permanently."

Because Ezra had gotten into drug-related trouble before, his parents thought it would be best to get him into some sort of treatment. He was enrolled as an outpatient at a local hospital's drug unit, although he would live at home.

After being expelled from school for drinking alcohol and selling marijuana, Ezra entered a treatment program.

"I went there every day," he says. "We'd do a group session each day, and I'd have classes there, too. And no, if you're going to ask if it helped me, it didn't. I'd come home from the treatment center each day and I'd keep hanging out with my friends, selling weed, smoking it, and drinking. I didn't care at all; I didn't want help. It's hard to understand unless you've gone through it yourself, I guess. But I resented other people trying to 'cure' me or help me. I didn't want to listen to them at all."

IN AND OUT OF TREATMENT

When Ezra was caught selling drugs to someone in his treatment class, it became apparent to those who knew him that he needed more serious care.

"I was put into a thirty-day evaluation for drugs and stuff," he says. "And after that, they said I had to stay on at this facility. When I was there, I had lots of problems. I still had the mindset that I wanted to drink and do weed. I didn't want to be there, but it wasn't a choice for me. This was required because I'd messed up at the other treatment place.

"You had to do your steps there, you know, your twelve steps. But I wasn't getting things done right. For one thing, I didn't like being confronted. See, that's a big thing in treatment, in groups. If people in the group don't think you're being honest, or you're being defensive or something, they'll call you on it.

"But I'd get mad at being confronted," he shrugs. "I didn't like it. And sometimes I'd make fun of some of the other people in the group. That's not good, either. Plus, I was still in the mindset where I wanted to smoke weed and drink, but the weed was the strongest urge."

After living away from home for three months at the treatment center, the staff had a meeting with Ezra and his parents. Since he was not accomplishing much, the staff felt he should be allowed to leave.

"I wasn't doing the steps," he admits. "My counselor wanted to help me by switching the steps around, the order, but still it wasn't working. I was getting a little better about the rules; I wasn't a problem. It's just that I wasn't getting much out of it.

"The solution was for me to go to Anthony, the school near me. The plan was for me to go there but have four alternative classes during the day. The other three periods I'd be mainstreamed with the other kids. So that's it—they let me loose."

NEW BAD BEHAVIORS

It was only a couple of weeks, says Ezra, until he started smoking marijuana again.

"My older sister had it," he says. "I knew she used it sometimes because once I saw it when I was looking in her car for a cigarette. I'd wait until she was downstairs or in the shower or something, and I'd look in her coat or her purse. So I found some, and I smoked it.

"It's funny how going back one time like that can trigger all the old behaviors. I forgot all about the twelve steps and treatment and all of that. And I started selling and using even more with the kids from Anthony. I was really into it. I had a pager, and I'd hang out down by the theater. Kids would page me a lot wanting to buy stuff.

"And being around that school more, I met more and more kids. I was getting invited to lots of parties on the weekends. And it seemed like alcohol was more and more interesting to me, you know? Like, weed was cool, and it had its advantages. Like, it was a lot easier to buy and sell; it was easy to put in your pocket or whatever.

"But weed started getting old—that's the best way I can explain it. I started really liking the feeling of getting drunk. It's a different feeling from getting high, I guess. So I started drinking more and more—not just on the weekends, either. My favorite drink was beer, I guess. I'd get a forty ouncer and that would be good. One and a half of those, and I'd be drunk. I liked that feeling, and it seemed like as time was going by, I was getting as addicted to alcohol as I was to weed."

MORE SCHOOL TROUBLE

Ezra was enjoying himself at school, although he was quickly getting the reputation of someone who "used."

"I came to school high sometimes," he says. "And I'd come with $150 worth of weed with me. And I drank at school; I'd just mix orange juice or pop with liquor and put it in a thermos or something. It wasn't like I was the only one doing that—it happens a lot at school. It seemed like the kids knew I used all the time. They didn't even ask if I was high—they knew I was every day. I know that the liaison at school knew I'd had problems at the schools I'd gotten kicked out of—he'd been around back when that pellet gun thing happened.

"I knew that the teachers or whatever were suspicious of me. They called me down to the office once, but I'd told someone to hold my weed for me. So they didn't catch me that time. But another time, this one girl who didn't like me went and told the liaison officer that I had a pipe and weed on me. So they called me down, and they found it. I got suspended for five days.

"When I came back from that suspension, there was a meeting with my parents and the staff and me. The school would let me come back but only if I would agree to being searched every time I came in the building. I'd have to go home on the bus every day,

Ezra admits to drinking at school, often mixing orange juice or pop with liquor and carrying it in a thermos.

too—no more hanging around after school. I was mad. I just walked out of the meeting. I was done there—no more Anthony. From there, yeah, it was just another alternative school. They kind of blended together after a while."

"WE DIDN'T TALK ABOUT A LOT OF THINGS IN OUR FAMILY"

Ezra acknowledges that he was a chronic troublemaker, yet he bristles at the notion that his parents could have been too trusting.

"It wasn't their fault," he says tersely. "It was me acting a certain way. It wasn't that they didn't care about me. I know they did. It's just that we just let things go in our family. My mom and dad would get mad at me for stuff, they'd ground me or take the phone away.

"But like that time when my dad came and got me after I'd been in lockup overnight—when I pointed that gun at him— no, he didn't say anything about it in the car. We just forgot about it, put it behind us; just let it be, we didn't talk about it. We didn't talk about a lot of things in our family, we just dropped them.

"But that doesn't mean they didn't enforce rules. I remember plenty of times they'd get mad at me for stuff. For a while it was like a constant thing, getting calls from school, from teachers, from liaisons, from police. I think at some point it was hard for them to know what to do with me.

"I remember my dad getting really mad once up at our cabin. It was about that time when I was really getting more into alcohol. I'd brought my best friend up there, too, and we'd gone into town and had gotten someone to buy us liquor at the store. We'd gotten

"We didn't talk about a lot of things in our family, we just dropped them," Ezra says about his family.

drunk in town and asked to be picked up and taken back to the cabin. I didn't think I was that drunk, but I was.

"In my dad's car, I was so out of it he could tell right off what the two of us had been doing. I got in trouble pretty good then and was yelled at. Plus, my friend had to leave the cabin and go back home to the city. So yeah, there were plenty of times I got in trouble. I'd get grounded or whatever. But if I did, I'd just leave. I didn't really care. It just didn't matter to me; at least, it didn't matter as much as it should have."

HOUSEBREAKING

Taking outrageous chances and doing things he clearly knew were wrong were other symptoms of Ezra's dependence on alcohol and drugs. During the summer between seventh and eighth grade, he and a friend came up with a dangerous scheme.

"We were just sitting under the bridge smoking, kind of wondering what we were going to do that night," explains Ezra. "He started to tell me about this house that he knew was empty. This kid—I think he knew him from school—was with his mom and dad in Italy or somewhere for the whole summer. And he knew where the key was to the house.

"So we walked over there and checked it out. We went inside and smoked some weed and started looking around. We found like a liquor cabinet or whatever, more than two hundred bottles of hard liquor. That was just in the kitchen. And I went in the kid's room and found some cash, like four hundred dollars; lots of CDs, tapes, stuff like that. And downstairs in the basement there were like fifty bottles of wines.

"Well, we decided not to keep this to ourselves. We thought we'd have a big party, invite like all the kids we knew. We ended up being at the house on and off for two weeks. We drank up everything—all the wine, all the hard liquor. I did a lot of drinking then. We'd take a bottle with us, drive around.

"There was a huge group of kids, but we'd leave sometimes and take bottles with us to other houses, to other parties. Before, the biggest parties I'd been to were like fifteen kids. But this was huge; and it never ended, not for two weeks!"

CAUGHT

In addition to the use of the family's home and liquor supply, Ezra admits that he and his friends did a great deal of vandalism.

"We trashed the place; that's pretty much it," he says. "We were drunk so much, and that's just what happened. We'd broken windows, we'd taken the TVs, radios, everything. Me? Yeah, I took a lot of stuff. I took CDs, the Nintendo, stuff like that. I sold a lot of it. Anyway, it seemed for a while like maybe we'd gotten away with it. It's pretty incredible when you think of all the activity that was going on in that house that nobody called the cops.

"But it turned out that I did get caught. What happened was someone at the party had carved a phone number in their wooden table. I'm not sure why, it was just the number of someone they were calling, I guess. Anyway, the cops who were investigating called the number and asked who called those people during that certain time, you know? Well, it got back to someone at the party, and then to me, since it was my party, sort of.

"I got called down at my alternative school—called down to the principal's office in October. They'd been called by the cops, and they wanted to talk to me. Anyway, I wasn't arrested, but I was supposed to go to court for the vandalism and stuff. I ended up being expelled from that school, too. They'd caught me with weed and with a razor blade in my wallet; I had that to cut up weed, you know? And I had also punched this one girl in the face. That's a long story; she started yelling at me in class and wouldn't get out of my face, and I hit her. Anyway, I got expelled."

Robbing Beer Trucks

Although many of the elements of Ezra's life changed, his way of life remained the same. He went from school to school, but it had no effect on how he acted.

"Nothing much was changing for me," he agrees. "I was in my usual routine, getting drunk or getting high, whichever. I was still selling weed."

As is the case with most teens who abuse alcohol, Ezra says that he had no difficulty obtaining alcohol.

"I stole some wine from my parents sometimes," he says. "And there were always kids who would buy it for you if you asked them to. Older kids, maybe friends of my older brother. And I'd take it sometimes out of the back of my brother's car; he kept some in there. And like I said, when I was up at the cabin, we'd just see who was going into a liquor store, and someone would always help out and get you some. People think it's so hard to get alcohol, like kids can't get it because they're too young to buy it—that's not true. You just don't buy it in stores, not personally. There's always someone willing to do it, always someone with a stash that you can steal from. It's not something that I'm proud of now, but it's the truth.

"There is a liquor store like two blocks from my house. And I've even robbed trucks there," he says. "I mean, the big Budweiser trucks or the MGD trucks would pull into the parking lot. When the guy gets out and goes into the store, you can just get stuff out

After Ezra ran away from the treatment center, social workers sent him to a Department of Corrections facility. "It was a little like jail," he says.

of the open truck. I took cases and cases out of there—probably like six times, at least. I'd put them in the trunk of my friend's car; he'd be there helping me."

TREATMENT

Ezra went to court early in 1997 for his part in the housebreaking incident. It was decided that the authorities would do a so-called Rule 25—a review of the problems that were on his records.

"They looked at the times I was kicked out of schools for selling or using drugs or fighting or whatever," he says. "And after looking at everything, they decided I should go to a treatment center, a live-in place.

"I ended up waiting like two months to get in; they can only take so many kids at a time, I guess. I started in February. It was an open setting—kids just walking around, playing pool, watching TV, stuff like that, a couple of classes each day, and an occasional group. There wasn't anything hard about it.

"Well, I was there two days. I got really mad in a group meeting; I was being confronted and I still didn't like that. Later I just got my coat and walked out—I just left! I walked to a mall nearby. I'd seen it when we drove to the treatment center. Anyhow, I caught a bus there, went back to my neighborhood. I went over to this one girl's house I knew, and I got drunk.

"I went back to my house the next day. My parents were at work, and the police picked me up. I guess they figured out where to look for me. Anyway, I got taken back to the treatment center.

"I hated it there; me and another guy and a girl decided to run away. It was two weeks later, and we left the center, walked over to the Amoco station where they have like a fixit place, you know? There were cars there waiting to be worked on with the keys still in them. So we just drove off. I drove the car; we headed back over to my neighborhood and started drinking.

"We ended up getting in a small accident. We were going around the lake and I hit a little patch of ice and the car went off to the side into a snowbank. We didn't want to stay there—we might get caught, you know? So we walked for a while, over to the library and hung out. I ran into some kids from Anthony, and we smoked a little weed with them.

"Anyway, we decided it was time to move. It was like eight o'clock at night, and we needed a car. We went through some cars, looked for one with keys. We found a van and took it. The other guy did the driving this time. Actually, it turned out that he wasn't any better at driving than I was. We were heading west, towards where he lived, and it was really, really dark out. We hit another patch of ice and went off the side of the road. We were still high, so we just stayed in the car and kind of slept. We got caught and got taken back to the treatment center."

To a Closed Environment

Again, Ezra and his two friends ran away from the treatment center. They stole another car from the Amoco parking lot and drove until they were caught by the police.

"This time they didn't just send me back to treatment," he says. "I was sent to a county work program, cutting wood and building fences for two weeks. It wasn't treatment, no. It was like a punishment. And I did that, and then ran again after a couple of weeks. I wasn't ready, you know? No one could tell me anything; I didn't want to participate. I wanted to be anywhere but there."

It was finally clear to social workers that Ezra needed a closed environment for his treatment, one from which he could not run away. He was assigned to a center north of the city.

"You couldn't walk away at all. There were twelve boys to a unit. It was a little like a jail, yeah. I mean, it was Department of Corrections; it said that on the door. It was partly like jail and partly treatment. It's like a big farm. There were eight units. Some were open units—the doors were unlocked, and kids could go to the public school nearby—but some were locked.

"That's where I was first. There was a computer man who had to let you in and out. You had to go past three big metal doors just to get to where I was. No way you could just stroll out and leave like at the other place. The rooms were pretty little, like maybe fourteen by twenty feet. There was a bed that was built into the wall, and a metal locker that was locked all the time. They had the key, I couldn't have access to the stuff unless they unlocked it. And there was a desk with a stool attached to it. And a toilet and sink."

Moving On

Ezra says that it was a relief when he was finally allowed to move to a more open unit.

"We didn't have to have our food in our rooms," he says. "It wasn't so much like a jail. In the open units, you went up to the lodge and ate with other kids. I made some friends there, got to know kids; so that was better. I felt more human. It really makes you think when you get your freedom taken away. It isn't like fun and games anymore. In those locked units, you can understand what it would feel like to be a prisoner, a convict, spending years and years behind bars.

"The time was a lot more structured than anywhere I'd been," he says. "No more wandering around playing pool or just hanging around with other kids. It seemed like every minute had to be accounted for."

What was a typical day like? It started very early, Ezra says with a grimace.

"You wake up at like six," he says. "And you eat breakfast and then go to school. When I was in the locked unit, the classes were right there. The school was challenging but not really difficult. I didn't have much problem with any of it. Then, at eleven, we went back to the unit and had lunch. Afterwards we had two more hours of school, and then we'd have a CT group—corrective thinking.

"That was where people would come up with issues from the past, things they were working on. Other people in the group would offer suggestions, help them out on what they could do the next time a situation came up or whatever. We all had to participate. And this wasn't my best thing from before—I hated being confronted about stuff.

"I wasn't good at first, even here. But I got better. I got into it, sort of grew into it, I guess."

BEING HOMESICK

"I was homesick," Ezra admits. "I was able to see my family twice a month and I really appreciated that. And when I got to the open unit, I could have home visits. That was twice a month, for a weekend."

Ezra says that his family did not treat him any differently when he came home, although he acknowledges that to his younger siblings it must have seemed especially strange.

"I don't know what they thought inside," he says. "When they looked at me, sitting at the dinner table or whatever, I don't know what they were thinking. But they were great—they just

Ezra's family has helped him recover. "We talked about why I was doing the things I did and what I needed . . . to help me stay sober and out of trouble."

treated me like a normal brother. I never thought I'd be so happy just to be treated as a regular kid!"

At the twice-a-week visits at the treatment center, Ezra and his parents talked a lot about the things that had happened over the past years.

"We talked about why I was doing the things I did and what things I needed—things I needed to help me stay sober and out of trouble," he says. "There was a lot of anger, a lot of tears at those meetings. I mean, it's obvious; these were emotional things we were talking about.

"I knew that if I was to get myself out of that center, I had to do a lot of hard work. Talking to my parents was part of that hard work, so was owning up to my mistakes, taking responsibility. I had to learn to be honest and to accept help—two things that I hadn't been doing. And my parents were really supportive, really fair."

Ezra says that his main motivation was wanting to leave. "I had to stay out of places like that," he says. "I wanted to go home."

Back Home

Ezra has been home for about six months, and he has not used alcohol or drugs during that time.

"I don't intend to," he says flatly. "I can't say I never will, but I can say that I don't want to. I know what kinds of things happen to me when I use, and I definitely don't want that. I want my freedom; I want to be home with my family.

"I have a job over at the mall in one of the clothing stores. I like it. It's nice to be making money on my own. I'm busy and that helps a lot."

Ezra is also glad that he is enrolled at Sobriety High. "I haven't been here nearly as long as some of the other kids," he says. "But they make you feel welcome. It's really small, so you can't just be a face in the crowd like at other schools. And all of us have had the same sorts of problems with alcohol and drugs or whatever. The teachers know all about it; they understand the kinds of pressures we have, so nothing gets swept under the rug. Everything is open—we can talk about everything.

"I've made a lot of friends here, and that's good for me. I still see some of my old friends, but they know I'm sober now, so they don't expect me to do the same stuff I used to with them. But with my friends from school, we sort of know what's OK and what's not. I spend a lot of time with these new guys.

"My family and I get along great now. My parents aren't as nervous anymore because I guess I haven't given them reasons to be. They trust me, and I like that. We communicate a lot, too. If they notice that I'm doing something that makes them uncomfortable, they say so and we talk about it. That's new for us, and it's helping, yeah."

"MY OWN WAY"

Ezra attends two types of meetings each week: Alcoholics Anonymous (AA) and Narcotics Anonymous (NA).

"That's one of the things you have to do at Sobriety High," he
explains. "And I do it. But really, I don't think the twelve steps of
AA is for everybody.

"For me, the part I get hung up on is the bit about turning
everything over to a higher power, or God, I guess. I say, just deal

*Enrolling in Sobriety High, attending AA and NA meetings, and finding a job
have helped Ezra stay clean and sober.*

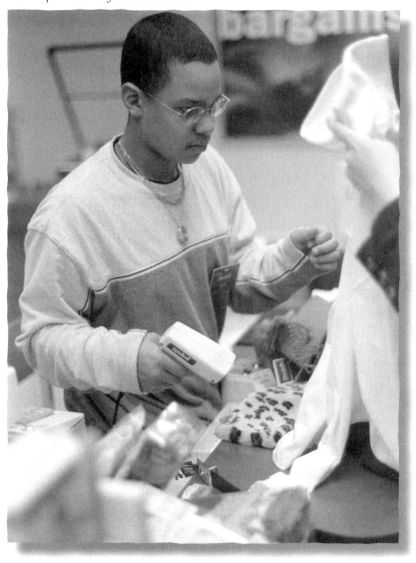

with it. I mean, I believe in God, of course, I do. But I think people should do stuff for themselves. I need to get sober myself; I need to get through that stuff myself. God can't do much for me if I'm not ready to take responsibility myself.

"Right now I need to make a choice to change. I made that decision back at treatment. And it's like I need to keep making that decision each day, each time I'm tempted or have cravings to go back to my old life. I believe in AA—I like the idea of the meetings and being supportive of each other. That's great. And I'll do that—I just don't follow the twelve steps myself." He shrugs, "I guess whatever works for me is the best thing, right?"

Melissa

"THAT WAS AUGUST 5, 1996. . . .
THAT WAS IT. I'VE BEEN SOBER
SINCE THEN."

Author's Note: Melissa, nineteen, is an alcoholic who has been sober for two and a half years. A longtime member of Al-Ateen (her father is also an alcoholic), she was always well aware of the dangers of drinking. Even so, she began drinking in high school and became instantly addicted. When talking to Melissa, it is easy to see how she was able to keep her drinking a secret from her family. By her own admission, she has always played the role of "good girl," eager to please and remarkably confident and poised. As she remarks, "Who would ever believe someone like me was capable of being such a wild drinker?" Now a sponsor and speaker with Alcoholics Anonymous, Melissa is eager to tell her story yet reluctant to have her photograph taken. "I don't want anyone who might be thinking of coming to a meeting seeing me and saying, 'Oh, she doesn't look like me; maybe I wouldn't fit in.' It's important that we don't put a face on our organization. It's not at all that I'm ashamed or unwilling to show my face—I do it all the time at meetings!"

The apartment is in a particularly lovely part of town and is situated off the road, hidden by large old maples and birches. Melissa answers the door immediately. She is an attractive nineteen-year-old with long reddish hair that she is trying, unsuccessfully, to tie back. She smiles, and with the confident air of a woman twice her age, welcomes me to her home in a surprisingly hoarse voice.

"I woke up with a real sore throat," she rasps. "I'm sorry I can't talk louder. But I'll try to give you as much of the details of my story as I can. Having listened to lots and lots of alcoholics tell their own stories, I can vouch for this: The details are the things you remember. They are what make the stories so real, so personal."

"My Mom Is a Great Human Being"

According to Melissa, her own beginnings were not as dramatic as many of the stories she has heard.

"I love my family," she says, pointing to a kitchen wall covered with snapshots. "You can tell, I guess. That's me there, in the middle of them all. I have a brother named Alex who is two-and-a-half years younger than I am. We have the same mom and dad. I also have two half sisters, one six and one almost four. They live with my dad and my stepmom in Phoenix.

"My parents divorced when I was three, and, for all intents and purposes, I was raised by my mother. I'm really lucky because she's absolutely great, my mom is a great human being. She's loving and patient and very, very kind.

"I don't know specifically why my parents divorced. I do know that my mom was seventeen when she married, and my dad was eighteen. And I was born a year later. Her explanation to me was that the things you look for when you are seventeen are often very different from what you look for as a woman. That makes a lot of sense to me.

"She has done a good job throughout my life making sure I knew that my dad loves me. She never bad-mouthed him, never bashed him. It would have been tempting, maybe, for they are not friendly—even now, so many years later. I know now that he did not pay child support for a long time. But all that was kept from me; her feelings toward him didn't have anything to do with her wanting me to have a good relationship with my father."

"I Was Just a Stubborn Kid"

Were there signs when she was young that she might be prone to alcoholism? Melissa thinks a moment and shakes her head.

"Not in that sense, not really," she says slowly. "I mean, I wasn't begging for sips of beer or anything like that. If I had to sum myself up in a phrase, I'd say I was a 'good girl.' I was good in school; I enjoyed playing school when I was little. I was organized, disciplined. I was the straight-A student, kind of nerdy, a teacher's pet.

"I did have this one character thing—in fact, I still do," she smiles. "I usually didn't want to do something unless I thought I could be the best in it. It might be a game, a class, whatever. It wasn't so much a school thing when I was little, I guess, but it happened in other activities.

"I remember when I was about seven, my mom wanted to have me take dance lessons. We walked into the studio and I saw some other little girls my age doing things I didn't know how to do. I mean, there would be no reason why I would know how to do those things because I'd never had a dance lesson before. But I got really upset. I didn't know how to do whatever it was they did, and that idea frightened me enough to where I started to cry. When I did that, we left. No more dance lessons. I was a stubborn kid, I guess."

RUNNING WITH THE MEAN GIRLS

It is difficult to imagine Melissa hanging out with the aggressive, mean girls in school, but that was her social group, she says.

"Yep, I was as mean as they came," she laughs. "That was middle school. That was me and Heather and Becky and Megan. We were mean to everybody except the kids who were picked on by the rest of the school. Those kids we left alone. I was always in the middle of the group; that's how you could find me. I'd be the one causing all the commotion, being the meanest.

"I'm not at all proud of that now. I wasn't nice, not kind. Not the person I'd like to be now. Tressa was a good example of someone we were mean to. We didn't like her—and don't ask me why. The only thing I can think of is that she wasn't in our group, but she wanted to be our friend; not mine, so much, but friends with the other kids in my group. She had made me mad back in fifth grade, I think, and I was busy holding a grudge. I could really carry a grudge a long time back in those days!

"Anyway, Tressa was sort of a late bloomer. She hadn't started getting her period like the rest of us. Well, one day in eighth grade, we heard that Tressa had started her period. So we stuck pads all over her locker, all over the place. We put up a big sign, too: Congratulations! Tressa Got Her Period Today! It was very embarrassing for her, of course. She was mortified. She knew we weren't doing it in fun; we were being malicious. I think that was the meanest thing we did."

"MY DAD IS AN ALCOHOLIC"

When Melissa was fourteen, she began going to Al-Ateen meetings. She had started seeing her father, who had moved to Phoenix, and her mother thought it was a good idea.

"My dad is an alcoholic," she says. "I can say that because he's an admitted alcoholic; he's been back out for seventeen years. That's most of my life. *Back out*—that means using again. He had been sober for a short period of time when I was younger but then relapsed. He's continued to use since then. It's been a lot of misery, a lot of time.

"I want to be clear about this: I love him. I mean, he's my dad. And he's done the best job with me that he knows how to do. But a lot of things have gotten in his way, especially his alcoholism."

Is he an abusive drunk? Melissa shakes her head.

"Not at all," she says. "But he's loud and scary when he's not drinking. He has a temper; he's a loud, scary guy, and he's at his absolute scariest when he's sober. That sounds backwards, I know, but it's true. You can almost feel the atmosphere in the room start to mellow when he drinks. He needs it; he just doesn't function without it. For him, it's beer. He'll sit down with a case of beer, about one a night. You just don't see my dad without a beer in his hand. That's how it is, and that's how it always was."

AL-ATEEN

"Anyway, my mom had been in Al-Anon for years, being the wife of an alcoholic. She thought it was a real good idea for me to get involved, too, especially since I was going out to visit him occasionally. So right after I came back from a visit, I went to my first meeting. And it helped a lot, helped for all of the things it was supposed to help for. Mostly, it helped me be all right for who I was and not be so concerned about taking care of everybody around me.

"See, I was always worrying when I was younger that I had to take care of him or the rest of them. It seems hard to believe that a child could feel so much responsibility toward a parent, but it happens a lot, I know. You do things like making sure Daddy's always happy; you try to be extra good, keep things nice and quiet, nothing loud or worrisome that he'll get mad about. You do everything you're told without having to be told twice.

"It works enough to keep the cycle going," she admits, "so it feels that I'm succeeding and nobody's getting yelled at. The problem is that somewhere in all that action, the person I was—the things I wanted for myself—get lost. So that's what Al-Ateen helped with."

Al-Ateen meetings have helped Melissa set priorities in her life.

SWITCHING FRIENDS

Melissa says that her experiences in Al-Ateen had resulted in her setting down a rule for herself.

"I was never going to drink," she says simply. "That was how I felt about it, probably because of what my dad had done and how his drinking had affected his life. I thought about how some of the kids I knew were starting to drink, and I made the decision that I would not be a drinker.

"As we were ready to start high school, a lot of my closer friends started drinking—those girls who, like me, had said they would never drink. The way I handled that was to switch friends. I started hanging around with the really good girls."

Melissa laughs. "It was funny, at first, me being a mean girl. I mean, they were a little distrustful of me at first—no wonder! Jenny, the girl I was especially close to in that group, tells me all the time how she was so afraid of me at first. It was like, 'What on earth is she doing with us?' But it seemed like the smartest thing to do. I was doing well in my classes, and high school was going along OK.

"But things went wrong," she says. "Goodness, it was just so simple that things went wrong."

"IT WAS LOVE, RIGHT AWAY"

As it turned out, the good girls enjoyed a bit of drinking, too. It wasn't a lot—perhaps only a beer, or maybe a beer and a half, at a party.

"They'd giggle a little, and that was that," says Melissa. "I look back and I don't understand it, how they did that. We'd go to parties, they'd drink a little bit. I remember thinking that there was no reason why I couldn't do that, too.

"I didn't pick up my first drink, as it turned out, until I was a sophomore in high school. It was at a party at the beginning of the year. It was right there in front of me, and I didn't even give it a thought. It was there, and I drank it, and it was love, right away. Not the taste, not at all. Just how it made me feel.

"You see," she explains, "I've got this horrible, diseased, sick brain. And it tells me—even today—all kinds of crazy things. A lot of the messages I get from my brain are really ugly. It's stuff like, 'You're not good enough' or 'People don't like you.' Sometimes it's 'You're crazy, you're fat, you're ugly.' Those kinds of things. I don't know where it comes from; I have no idea. I wasn't taught those things when I was little.

"But that stuff is there. As long as I can remember, it's been there. I don't think there was ever a kid who got more love than I did. But that's me; that's what's in my brain. As a result, I tend to be shy—as shy as they come. I hide that by overcompensating; I don't let anyone know how unsure of myself I am. I pretend I'm in complete control. I assault people with my personality! But inside, even right now, I'm afraid. It's better now than it was, but it's still there.

"Anyway, back to my drink. I had that first one—a shot of tequila gold—and all of a sudden I wasn't shy. It was like those things my brain had been telling me weren't there anymore. And so I had another shot and another. And man, I was the best-looking thing in that room! No one was funnier, no one was smarter. And that's how I really felt."

MORE AND MORE

Melissa explains that that was the first of many times she would get drunk. But the attraction of getting drunk was neither the taste of the drink nor the fun of being silly in a group of friends.

"It was to be someone else," she says bluntly. "That's it. And believe me, I was someone else when I drank. You can kind of picture it—the kind of parties my new friends and I were going to. The room would be full of student government people, the homecoming queens, the student council secretaries with their little single beers—maybe one and a half, if they were feeling really wild. And there I'd be, and their mouths would be agape. I was wild; I was uninhibited; I felt like throwing punches. I was always ten times crazier than the craziest person there.

Melissa says she didn't drink because she liked the taste. She drank because she could act like a different person under alcohol's influence.

"From that point on, I got drunk every time I drank. And I did all kinds of scary things. I'd black out and then wake up on the back of a motorcycle, barely hanging on. I don't remember before or after, just like a minute memory—me waking up and saying, 'Who's driving; what's going on?' I remember looking over the shoulder of the guy driving—who was as drunk as me—seeing how fast he was going.

"And the more I drank, the more frequently these scary things were happening. As it happened, I was a very mean drunk, not a happy person. I know there are those people who get happy and generous when they drink, but that was definitely not me."

LIVING THE LIE

How did she feel about her drinking? Didn't she worry that she might be following in her father's footsteps?

"The thing was," Melissa says, choosing her words carefully, "I was sort of telling myself a lie—one that I really believed for a time. Part of the lie was that since I was attending Al-Ateen meetings, that would somehow save me from becoming an alcoholic; that I could have all that behavior, drink all that tequila or whatever, and I wouldn't be an alcoholic because I went to Al-Ateen like I somehow knew the secret.

"And I also told myself that this was just recreation. As long as I could keep bringing my good grades home, and as long as I fooled the adults around me, then whatever I did was OK."

Melissa sighs, "It stopped working at some point, sure. It was getting more and more obvious to people around me, to my friends, and it was carrying over into other parts of my life. I started off with this whole group of friends and great people in my life, and one by one I either scared them off or alienated them so much that they had no alternative but to stop being my friends anymore.

"Sure, I was still going to the parties, but very few people were interested in being around me. I had four friends as it turned out— four girls who stuck by me through high school; four girls who are still my friends today. That's Danielle, Bri, Kristina, and Jenny. I don't know how they did it; it must have been really difficult for them to be my friend back then."

"IT WAS EMBARRASSING"

While her friends were loyal, Melissa says, they certainly did not encourage her to drink.

"Not at all," she insists. "For a while they were somewhat concerned; they'd just kind of treat it as 'Keep an eye on Melissa.' But after a while it was more than concern—they were more like on duty, watching out for me. That was how it worked.

"You have to understand, though, that a great deal of my drinking was when I was alone. That party aspect of it was just a fraction of the alcohol I was consuming. Or even if I was at a party, I'd hide so that no one knew how much I was using. Really, I'd hide in the shower or in a bedroom somewhere. I knew that I was drinking so much more than other people, so much more than I should, but it was embarrassing to show anyone how much I was consuming."

She reaches both hands behind her head, trying to rework the elastic holding her hair.

"After a certain point I couldn't deal with anyone without having at least a little alcohol in my system. That means my family, school, my friends, work. And it wasn't as hard as it sounds. I kept my stash in shoeboxes right in my closet, way up high on a shelf—it looked like nothing. You'd never think to look there; all the boxes had shoes in them but that one, where I had a bottle of tequila at all times.

"Yeah, tequila," she smiles ruefully. "That was my drink; I stayed with it. I drank other things, of course, but that was definitely my favorite. I found myself needing more and more, too. Goodness, I'd carry two pints of tequila in my purse. That was standard.

"Sometimes I'd be on the verge of passing out, but there was always that extra little bit at the bottom of the bottle that I'd need to finish off. I couldn't stand to have it there, you know? Or even more gross, the next morning I'd be finishing off people's empties. I'd have the garbage can nearby, so it seemed like I was cleaning up if I got caught. But I'd be filtering out cigarette butts just to get at what was at the bottom of the glass. That's the kind of stuff I did."

"THERE WAS NO 'DRUNK ENOUGH'"

The amount that Melissa required to silence the voice in her brain increased as the weeks and months went by.

"After a while there was no 'drunk enough' anymore," she admits. "There was just not enough alcohol that I could put in my body that would make that brain shut up. That voice, that paranoia—whatever you want to call it—that feeling that everyone was better than I was, was winning.

"I know everybody has that voice to some extent. I know I'm not the only one, but I think most people can deal with that voice better. That's the big difference between why I felt the need to drink and other people maybe didn't. I don't know how to deal with life—I guess that's it in a nutshell.

"And boy, I was drinking an awful lot of tequila just trying to stay ahead of the voice. Of course, this is when I was fifteen, sixteen, seventeen. I wasn't old enough to buy my own, but that wasn't a problem. I knew five or six people with fake IDs who could get it for me. I tried to keep it a secret that it was all for me, sure. But it's easy when you're making a big order; you can pretend it's for a lot of people. And hey, I'm a little girl from the suburbs! Why would anyone think I'd be a problem, right? I usually said it was for a party. And if worse came to worse and I couldn't get anyone to buy it, I'd just show up at a party. But no one else I knew drank as much as I did, so I'd have to bring my own just in case there wasn't enough."

"WHAT A BURDEN IT MUST HAVE BEEN"

Melissa's family was unaware of her problem, though her brother grew more and more suspicious that there was something wrong, she says.

"My brother ended up figuring it out," she says sadly. "I feel bad about that; he always looked up to me. I came home stinking, stumbling, ridiculously drunk, and he saw me on occasion. Mom would be asleep; I was such a 'good girl' she never worried about me.

"Alex was the only one that suspected, and what a burden it must have been for him, you know, the wondering, 'Should I tell because she might hurt herself, or should I be loyal and keep the secret?' That's a bad position to have put him in. It got to the point, after a while, that he would wait up for me. And meanwhile, he was going to the same Al-Ateen and Al-Anon meetings as I was.

"My mom was unaware the whole time," she says. "In fact, the first time she found out was after I'd been sober for two days! There were clues, of course, but she had no reason to look for them. My grades went down. Really, by the end of junior year

Melissa had little difficulty hiding her drinking from her family.

that was the worst. Where before I'd had mostly A's, a sprinkling of B's, I gradually went down to C's, maybe a B or a D. But it's easy to say, 'Oh, that was really a hard class,' or something like that."

ALMOST CAUGHT

Asked whether there was a time when she was almost caught by her mother, Melissa nods.

"Once, yes. Understand that I never came home drunk, at least at the beginning. I assumed she would catch me, and I didn't want that. But I remember one time being so drunk—I don't know even how I got home—but I was crawling up the front steps on my hands and knees. I was thinking, 'I'm so sick, I'm going to be in such huge trouble.'

"I got myself through the front door, and she was up—my worst nightmare. She was never up that late! But I walked in, and, let me tell you, I was covered with liquor. I stunk. I could smell me, that's how bad I stunk. She said, 'Honey! You don't look very good.'

48

"I told her that I'd had some bad Chinese food. I don't know why I said that, but it just came out of my mouth. And the minute I heard myself say it, I'm like, 'That's so stupid; now you're going to get caught for sure!' But she bought it. So after that, if I had to come home drunk, I didn't worry as much about it. Most of the time I'd just call and say I was staying over at my friend's.

"She didn't even know I was smoking—that's how much I had her fooled. I'd just tell her she was smelling someone else's smoke on me. She'd say, 'Honey, you smell smoky.' And I'd just say, 'Well, you know Bri smokes.' And that would be that. My mom was so in the dark about me, I had her so fooled that she would never think such a thing of her daughter as she was a drunk."

"Everything Accelerated Incredibly"

Her father and stepmother were no more aware of her drinking problem than was her mother, Melissa says.

"I was out there visiting; it was about three weeks before I got sober," she remembers. "It was there in Phoenix that everything accelerated incredibly for some reason. One thing was that there was a liquor cabinet—I was just obsessed! I had free rein on it; I didn't really worry at all that he'd discover bottles missing because he almost never used it. Like I said, he's a beer drinker.

"I'd wait until my stepmother, Janet, would go somewhere, and I was in business. I only needed like ten minutes alone in the house. I'd take the liquor as quickly as I could and drink until they got home. Things started getting worse. At that point I was just drinking to maintain some sort of 'not-shaking, able-to-deal-with-people' front. Actually, that was when I looked most normal, when I was just about passed-out drunk. It was then that people around me thought I was chatty, personable. Otherwise, I was antsy and really uncomfortable.

"I look at some of those pictures on the wall there," she says, pointing, "and I'm amazed at the difference. There are actually no pictures up there when I was at the height of my drinking—I didn't want to have my picture taken with my friends and family. That was the only time in my life when I would have refused, I think. But there are a few up there where I was definitely drinking. I look so puffy, so sick. Too skinny, yeah, but just puffy. I look unhealthy, and I was definitely taking less and less time with how I looked each day."

A Thought From Out of Nowhere

When she returned from her visit to Phoenix, Melissa spent the next week at what she describes as a week-long party.

"It was at my friend Bri's house," she says. "It was a party that just kept going. Music, food, drinks, just all kinds of stuff. My friends had so much fun; I don't remember it as being fun at all—isn't that strange? I remember maybe twenty minutes out of the whole week. Otherwise, I stayed drunk the whole time.

"I went home a couple of times, just to change clothes, I guess. I don't remember it. I even went to work once, I think. But most of the time I was at Bri's, staying drunk—drinking and drinking when my friends didn't even have an idea of how much I was drinking. At one point Jenny did try to take my bottle away from me, and I took a swing at her. My best friend! That's how bad it got."

At the end of that week Melissa became sick—more sick than she had ever been before.

"I shook all day, I had cold sweats," she says. "I felt horrible. Things were getting worse, almost by the hour. No amount of alcohol that I drank was enough any more; I was realizing that I could no longer satisfy the need.

"I remember I was sitting in my friend's shower, hiding because I didn't want the rest of them to see that I was drinking. And all of a sudden out of nowhere comes this thought. It was as clear as anything: You're an alcoholic like your dad. That's exactly what I heard in my brain."

A Plan

Melissa says that was the first moment she ever really thought of herself as an alcoholic.

"It's funny now because saying this, I can see that I was an alcoholic all along," she says. "I can see the signs so clearly. But then, I was in the middle of it, living it. And it really didn't hit me until then, sitting in the shower drinking. The voice wouldn't go away, either. So I made a plan for that night.

"This is an important part of my story, this part here," she stresses. "Because it shows just how bad I really was—that I could be thinking that but still not kick my butt enough to quit drinking. Because my plan was to drink that night—drink and drink and drink until I died. That was the plan.

"I knew I had enough liquor in my stash that I could do that. Everyone would think it was an accident, I was sure of that. It seemed to me, sitting there, that it was a great plan. So anyway, that night I drank. Not glassfuls, no—right from the bottle, the way a tough girl drinks!"

Melissa laughs humorlessly. "Anyway, I obviously didn't drink myself to death that night. I actually passed out very, very early that night—far earlier than I usually did. And the way I reacted to that? I just kept drinking. Any normal person, you'd think, would say, 'Wow, my life's out of control. I better do something.' Not me. It was full steam ahead for me."

A Conference Among Friends

By that time, Melissa says sadly, she was down to four friends— the only friends she had left. But they were concerned about her, and they let her know it.

"We had sort of a conference," she says. "They'd been talking about me, and they kind of elected Bri to be the one to talk for them. They were afraid for me and worried about what was going on.

"I apologized, first thing. I made it this weak little apology, and I told them I was sorry that I scared them so much. And I promised them that I was never, never going to drink again. And they believed me. And really, I believed me, too. It was the first time we had had words about my drinking, the first time it was really out in the open. So I gave a promise.

"I don't think they were being gullible, believing me. Like I said before, anyone looking at the situation would think, 'Sure, good, she's finally come to her senses. Having her friends intervene in her life like this after being so scared, this is the happy ending to the story.'"

What exactly was it that scared her friends so much?

"A lot of it was my dangerous behavior—the screaming, the taking risks, like on that motorcycle. I was in a relationship with a boy that was awful. I look back on it now, with the giant public screaming matches we'd had, and I say, 'Who was that girl?' Dave—that's the boy—had a way of reacting to my craziness with more craziness. I mean, I love him—he's great—but we're the wrong two people to be together. My friends saw this, they saw how much I hated my life. They could tell how much I hated myself, too.

"I was miserable; I never smiled," she recalls. "The happy, confident drunk wasn't there for long, not like that very first time I drank. This was a routine with me—we'd go to a party and I'd say, 'I'm not going to drink at all tonight.' Then I'd drink and I'd say, 'But I'm not going to finish this bottle.' And then the bottle would be gone and I'd say, 'I'm not going to start another one.' And so on, down the line. Lots of promises, lots of lies."

"THAT WAS IT"

Melissa says she had every intention of keeping her promise to Bri and her other friends. She went without alcohol for three days, she says, and on the third night she was going to be the designated driver when they all went to a party.

"I'd never been the sober cab person before," she smiles. "That was a new one for me. So we walked into the party; we all walked in together. There was a cooler right by the door, and it didn't even occur to me not to pick up a beer. It didn't even occur to me.

"Well, I drank half of it down in one swallow. My friends got so mad! And I got mad back. I told them, 'Listen, I'm not going to go without drinking the rest of my life. I've got to learn how to drink socially without getting drunk.' I told them that I wouldn't even finish that beer I had in my hand, and I definitely wouldn't have another. But I snowballed them.

"I finished my little speech to them, drained the first beer, and picked up a second—all in about four seconds' time. And then Bri started to cry. They all made a big scene, all talking at once; and then they took me home."

Melissa smiles. "That was August 5, 1996," she says. "That was it. I've been sober since then."

"HONEY, WRONG ROOM!"

She did not argue with Bri and the others when they took her home. As it happened, her behavior had frightened her, too.

"For whatever reason, I'd had all these consequences, and I was still picking up the beers," she says. "It was like I didn't have a chance against it, and I was realizing that. I was scared, yeah. And the next day I walked into my first AA meeting.

"It was kind of funny—I'd been going to that same building for Al-Ateen and Al-Anon for years," she laughs. "And when I walked

When Melissa entered AA, she realized it might be her last chance to save herself.

into that AA meeting, a lot of the guys recognized me—we'd see each other going in and out, you know? When I walked into the room, some of them were like, 'Honey, wrong room!' It was like I was in a parallel universe or something.

"The room was full of old men. That's not how all AA meetings are, but that one has always been attended by the older guys. I cried through the whole meeting; I was shaking, and my knees were hitting the bottom of the table where I sat. I was really scared. I couldn't believe that this was my life, that this was me. It was the last thing I was ever going to be, an alcoholic. And yet, there I was.

"I did what they told me to do. I was so desperate. It seemed like my last shot, I guess you could say. I mean, if I lied now to these people, I was doomed. And they told me to do some pretty important things. Today it doesn't seem like a lot, but then it did. Number one? Go to ninety meetings in ninety days. I did eighty-seven; I was sick for a couple of the days and out of town for another.

"But I went all the time. I attended different meetings, different sites. You don't have to go to the same group, no. I think the reason I moved around so much at first was because I was scared of people in general. I figured I could walk in as a new person once, and then I'd never have to see those people again."

"Something Bigger than You"

Melissa explains that one of the first things that happened at AA was that she got a sponsor.

AA's 12 steps have helped Melissa realize the importance of a higher power in her life.

"My first sponsor was Sarah, one of my roommates here," she says. "It's a very incredible relationship. The idea of a sponsor is that she's the one I call first, when I need support, when my brain is saying those crazy things. I could call her even if it were the middle of the night. The understanding is, of course, that she's been through the same things herself, so she gets it.

"It was a struggle early on, sure. At first, that first month, I wanted to get drunk so much! It was horrible. But back then I had none of the tools—the tricks, whatever you want to call them—that I have today. I had no idea at first of how to pick up the phone, or pray, or go to a meeting."

What about the religious aspect of AA? Do the members all believe in the same thing?

"Oh, no," she says. "Not at all. I mean, a big part of my life today is contact with the god of my understanding. In no way does AA try to coerce you to believe in a certain thing. Hey, if someone had told me when I walked into AA for the first time that I had to believe in this god and call god by this name or that name, I'd have left. That wasn't for me. My beliefs don't have to be in alignment with anyone else's, and that's always true. It's no different than me saying that nothing I tell you is a reflection of AA as a whole. It's just me, my experience.

"It's like that with God, my perception of God in my life. I know now that without some God in my life, I make very strange, very awful decisions. I found that out after AA was in my life. What seems to be an important part of the twelve steps of AA is that you understand that there is something bigger than you out there. I mean, you can call that God if you want; you can call it quantum physics—that's a force bigger than me. You can worship or not. Me, I don't go to church. That may change sometime, but today I don't go."

"That Would Seem Pretty Ungrateful"

Asked when she would consider herself cured, Melissa looks baffled.

"I can't imagine ever being done with AA," she says. "I hope I never am. Maybe forty years from now I won't be going to as many meetings each week, but who knows? My sponsor Heidi still does three meetings a week and so does her sponsor.

"I mean, thinking about it, I'd hope my attendance doesn't go down," she muses. "Gosh, that would seem pretty ungrateful

Melissa feels that AA will continue to be a major part of her life, and now she is even acting as a sponsor for other new members.

of me, I think. I think I'd always need it; a big part of my sobriety today is giving to other people.

"One of the best things in my life is the fact that I am a sponsor now—I've got sponsees of my own now. I work with them Sunday and Monday as well as Tuesday afternoons. I get so much out of being a sponsor—it's what I have to do to stay sober today.

"Those crazy messages my brain sends me are still there, after all. They aren't as loud all the time, but they're there. But when I'm having a particularly hard time with those thoughts, or if I'm having a rotten day, I just go to a meeting, chase down some newcomers and introduce myself. Working with new members, with my sponsees, I'm giving to them what was given so freely to me when

I walked in the door the first time. It's like I'm a vessel: My sponsors and other people have thrown me their good stuff, and I throw it back out to other people. I owe this tremendous debt."

"I'll Tell You About Luck"

Melissa knows she has been very fortunate in her life so far.

"I've got a great family who loves me," she says. "I've got great roommates, and I enjoy school. And even though my four best friends from high school are sort of all scattered now—everyone in school in different places—we still are close. We still keep in touch."

"And lucky?" she laughs. "I'll tell you about luck. About nine months after I got sober, I was so confident in myself that I went on a senior year spring break trip to Cancun!"

She rolls her eyes. "If one of my sponsees told me she was going to do that, I'd beg her to reconsider. I mean, it worked out OK—more than OK—but it wasn't the most conducive environment for staying sober. A cesspool, yeah. But I went to AA meetings there in Cancun; and, as it turned out, I probably am the only one of the kids on the trip who remembers everything that happened!"

Melissa is quick to add that she does not see drinking as a bad thing at all.

"I really don't," she insists. "I think there's something really wrong when I do it, yes. But I've got normal friends for whom a drink or two is an OK part of their lives at a party or whatever. It can be a fine thing, just not for me, not at all."

Joe

"I'M AN ALCOHOLIC. . . . I
SHOULDN'T BE ALLOWED
ANYWHERE NEAR THE STUFF. BAD,
BAD THINGS HAPPEN TO ME WHEN
I DRINK. I'VE SCREWED UP SO
MANY TIMES, MY FAMILY IS
RELUCTANT TO SEE ME. I KNOW
MY MOM LOVES ME, BUT I'VE TRIED
THEIR PATIENCE TOO MANY TIMES."

Author's Note: Joe, eighteen, has been an alcoholic and a drug user for as long as he can remember. To blame, he says, is the small rural town in which he grew up and the lack of anything more creative to do than get high. He is a moody young man but ultimately likable; the anger that sometimes surfaces often seems directed as much at himself as anyone else. Joe has been through treatment a number of times but has always re- lapsed. This time, he says, he is through drinking for good; legal problems stemming from his drinking have complicated his life. But even though his intentions are good, Joe seems to have a problem following through on his goals. Without a base of support from his family or a group such as Alcoholics Anonymous, Joe's sober future seems uncertain.

Although it is almost noon on a sunny autumn Wednesday, Joe is having a great deal of trouble keeping his head up. His white Adi- das cap is pulled down low, hiding the small blue teardrop tattoo on the side of his right eye.

"I stayed up real late last night," he says hoarsely, his voice raw. "I wasn't drinking or nothing. I just was hanging out with some friends. I'm not used to being up this early usually. I'm sorry it's tak- ing me so long to get going here. I guess I'm more talkative at night."

That, he admits, has been his problem throughout most of his adolescence. His late-night activities, including heavy alcohol and drug use, have undermined his attempts to do well in school, to have a strong family relationship, and to maintain supportive and caring friends.

"I'm an alcoholic," he says simply. "I shouldn't be allowed anywhere near the stuff. Bad, bad things happen to me when I drink. I've screwed up so many times, my family is reluctant to see me. I know my mom loves me, but I've tried their patience too many times.

"It's coming up on Thanksgiving in a couple weeks, and I was hoping to go to my grandmother's house—see my family. But I'm pretty sure my stepfather isn't too interested in seeing me. And you know, I don't want a big fight or a scene. It seems like my life has been like this a lot lately."

EARLY TIMES

Joe is originally from California; he and his family moved to the Midwest when he was five.

"My mom and dad got divorced when I was about three," he says. "I really don't remember much about stuff that early in my life. I know my mom used to drink and that my dad did lots of drugs. But my dad was pretty much out of the picture when I was growing up. I don't know what he did for a living or anything.

"My mom met my stepdad there in California; he was in the Marines out there. The two of them—plus my younger sister and me—we had a pretty OK life, I guess, at least at first. I remember doing real normal stuff like playing ball. I did all the fun little sports when I was young. I know I liked being active.

"But I also remember that my parents were drinking quite a bit. I can think back when I was little, how they would be arguing all the time. I'd be upstairs crying at night, listening to them. It was scary. They'd yell, throw stuff. I'd just scream up there, but they didn't hear me—too loud themselves, I guess. Sometimes my stepdad would even hit my mom. When that happened, my mom would take my sister and me, and we'd go off in the car to sleep at a rest area or something."

Joe says that he has to give his parents credit, however, because they decided they needed to stop drinking.

"They just stopped," he shrugs. "I don't know exactly how. I don't think it was any one thing that got them to stop; if it was, they didn't ever say anything to me. I think they knew they were headed for trouble if they kept it up, you know? Like if they were going to be drinking and fighting, their marriage wasn't going to last very long.

"So they just stopped, cold turkey. They cleaned up their act, just used willpower or whatever. They didn't go to meetings like Alcoholics Anonymous or anything. Just boom, straight, like that."

He claps his hands once for emphasis and shifts in his chair.

CHILDHOOD DRINKING

But while his parents were sorting out their drinking problems, Joe says, his were just beginning.

"When I was a little kid I had beer lots of times, me and my friend. We used to steal beer out of the fridge when my parents were having parties. This was before they stopped drinking, you know? Anyway, we used to throw it around outside, back and forth, until it exploded. We thought that was really cool. That was before we were brave enough to taste some.

"When we finally drank some, we both decided the taste was pretty nasty. When you're eight or nine, I guess that's normal. But I drank my can down, all the way down. That's kind of rare, I think. I guess I knew it would give me a buzz, so I didn't care about the taste. Maybe even back then I was an alcoholic and didn't know it, huh? I mean, most kids would have said, 'No way, the taste is horrible.' But for me, the high was worth it, even when I was a little kid.

"Anyway, that first time, my mom came walking in the garage where me and my friend were drinking. She's like, 'What have you got there?' And she just took it away from us. She didn't freak out or anything because most little kids experiment with beer, I guess. And like I told you earlier, this was before my mom and dad stopped drinking, so she wasn't as zeroed in on drinking as a bad thing."

On the contrary, as Joe remembers it, that first episode of drinking was a positive thing.

"It was a good experience," he says. "From then on, every chance I got I'd steal some beer. And it wasn't very hard back then because my mom and dad kept it in the garage. It was always easy to grab a couple of cans."

"HE WOULDN'T BELIEVE ME"

When his parents stopped drinking, things became calmer around his house for a while, Joe says. But as time went by, the yelling started again—but this time it was Joe and his stepdad.

"There was all kinds of trouble between him and me," Joe says bitterly. "This was when I was like ten or eleven, I guess. He started getting mad at me, treating me like he didn't believe me. Like, I'd come home from school and he'd ask me where my homework was. I told him I didn't have any. See, I got it done in class. But instead of just letting it go, he made a big deal out of it. He wouldn't believe me—he acted like I was lying to him all the time or being lazy. So there'd be fights, and he'd ground me."

It was at this time that Joe began drinking more often and became a drug user as well.

"I smoked weed," he says. "The first time I did it I was with this same friend that I drank with. We poked a hole in a pop can, put a choke in the side. That's kind of like making a do-it-yourself pipe. My friend knew how to do that stuff, and he taught me."

As with the first time he drank beer, Joe was radically affected by the marijuana.

"I had three big hits, and then I blacked out," he says. "I was really, really high. I mean, a lot of times you hear people talk about their first time, and they say they didn't feel anything. But that wasn't me! I started walking home from my friend's house, and I was having hallucinations. I started freaking out, thinking my friend's mother was sitting in her van watching us. I was so scared!

"We spent like a half hour or more just lying there in the snow, hiding. I kept saying, 'There she is, she's looking right at us!' But see, she wasn't there at all. So after a while, we realized that what I was seeing wasn't a van but a big snowbank.

"And the hallucinations didn't stop there, either. I went home and thought the bed was eating me alive. Every time I closed my eyes, I worried I was going to die. So I jumped up, took a shower, and jumped into bed with my mom; I just told her I was having a bad dream. I ended up taking like four showers that night!"

"IT WAS WHAT WE SAW"

Despite his young age, Joe says, he continued to use alcohol and marijuana after that, becoming increasingly dependent on both substances.

"See, the way I figure it, I didn't have much of a chance against either one of those substances," he says. "First of all, I think I was born an addict—an alcoholic—whatever. It's not the drugs, it's not the booze—it's what you do with that stuff that makes you become an alcoholic or an addict. Me, I don't process liquor right, or drugs either for that matter. It just does bad stuff to me.

"And second, besides being that kind of person that gets addicted to things like alcohol and drugs, I grew up in an environment where that's all there was. I'm from a little tiny town, and man, people who think that we all live clean out in the country are kidding themselves. There's lots of weed and booze. I think there's more drinking in little towns, maybe more weed, than even in the city! Maybe cities have more acid and crack, stuff like that; I don't know, because we got that in the country, too. But man, I knew more alcoholics from little towns, more addicts. It's incredible.

"My town had a gas station, a liquor store, but not much else. And the nearest town wasn't much bigger. And the kids that were teenagers when I was growing up, when I was ten or so, they were all users. Drugs and alcohol—they all used. My generation—my friends and me—we looked up to those guys.

"I hate going back there because it reminds me of how I let those guys control us. It was what we saw, man," Joe says, his voice growing tight with emotion. "When we went to the park to play, we saw kids drinking beer, throwing their empties around the playground. Drug stuff, too—it's just the way it was."

MANIPULATING HIS PARENTS

What about Joe's parents? Weren't they aware that he was using drugs and alcohol from his behavior?

"They had no clue," he says quickly. "No clue. I'm a smart person; I know how to be sneaky. I can sneak out of the house when I hear my stepdad snoring. I knew how to get behind my parents' backs. Sure, once in a while they'd catch me sneaking out—maybe I was going to go out with friends and drink or whatever—but they didn't know why I was sneaking out.

"So they'd put little traps in the door sometimes. They'd rip a little piece of paper and put it up high, so you couldn't see it. And when you left at night, the little piece would flutter down and that would prove you'd gone out, right? Anyway," he says, smiling, "it was stuff like that. It got to where I just looked for the little piece of paper. I'd see it fall, and I'd put it back.

"Maybe as time went on they suspected I was experimenting a little," he admits. "But there was never any proof that I was drinking and using drugs. If there had been, things might not

Joe doesn't like to visit his hometown because it reminds him of the many wasted days he spent drinking beer and taking drugs.

have gotten out of hand—who knows? I just told my parents that I was going to be out with friends. All kids are kind of vague like that.

"And the money? That came from my parents. I'd tell them I was going to do something with friends, like someone was going to drive us to a movie or something, and they didn't know. They'd just hand over ten bucks—they didn't know they were supplying me. And I'd blow it on weed or booze or whatever."

Joe bristles at the suggestion that his parents were shirking their responsibilities where his well-being was concerned.

"That's not true," he says stiffly. "It wasn't as though they didn't care. I know my mom cared a lot, they both probably did. When I'd go out, she'd always ask me where I was going. They'd say, 'Check in if you're going to be late,' or 'What time will you be home?' All the normal stuff. I think if they made a mistake, it was just believing me when I told them stuff."

"Lots of Stuff Was Going Through My Head, and It Wasn't School"

As Joe's use of drugs and alcohol increased, his performance in school suffered. By sixth grade his grades had dropped noticeably.

"Just down the tubes," he admits. "The more I was drinking and stuff, the harder it was to pay attention in class. I seemed to be tired all the time, and I'd fall asleep right during school. Or else I'd be paranoid—that was the weed—thinking other people were watching me or talking about me. Yeah, lots of stuff was going through my head, and it wasn't school.

"Seventh grade was even worse. The work was really hard, and I was using and drinking and not concentrating at all. I flunked every class—every single class I took all year. F, F, F, F," he laughs humorlessly. "I'd had my share of D's the year before. Before that, I'd been a really good student. So this was a real turnaround for me.

"My parents assumed it was a phase. I mean, there are kids who just hit bottom at certain ages, just get into a major slump. So I guess they figured that was what was happening to me. What got me, though, was how some of my friends were able to keep getting OK grades. These were some of the same guys I was drinking with or smoking weed with, but they weren't bottoming out like I was.

"But that's what I mean about an addictive personality," he explains. "It was me, not the substances I was abusing."

He thinks about that for a few moments. "My parents went to school at the end of seventh grade, had a conference with my teachers. They agreed to let me go into the eighth grade as long as I changed to a different type of class. It was a really small one, not like special ed, but remedial. There were only like eight or nine kids in there, so we got a lot of personal help. It helped a little, but not too much, to tell you the truth."

EXPANDING HIS DRUG USE

Joe says that his use of alcohol and marijuana continued, perhaps increasing, in eighth and ninth grade. He even drank in school, bringing beer from home.

"I'd put it in my locker—just put it in my tote bag and put it in there," he says. "I'd usually drink during lunch. I'd empty out a Mountain Dew can or whatever and fill it with beer, drink it right in the cafeteria. Nobody knew a thing about it, at least no teachers. I was considered a nice mellow guy then, not wild or anything. I didn't cause any problems, so I wasn't noticed.

Because Joe was not considered a troublemaker, no one paid close attention to his behavior, and he was able to get away with drinking at school.

"I still liked smoking weed sometimes, but not during school. It made me paranoid, so it wasn't as pleasant as being a little buzzed from the beer. But in ninth grade I kind of hooked on to a different drug that changed things for me.

"This friend of mine, Phil, was diagnosed as hyperactive. They prescribed this drug Ritalin for him, and he brought some of the pills to school one day. He told me I ought to try one of them, so I took two. I felt really good—I mean *really good!*

"It was such a difference for me, too. Like before, I'd always been really shy, really quiet around other people. I was afraid to stand in front of the class to do a report or whatever. I was even afraid to stand in front of people in a baseball game and hit the ball. I liked the games, I just didn't like being the focus of attention or whatever.

"But the Ritalin got rid of all that. I could talk to anybody; the shyness was gone. I'd talk to my teachers, make plans for things I was going to get done for school. It was just incredible! After that, I got some pills from Phil every day. I took three or four each day."

LOTS OF PARTIES

Joe says that simply being more confident and outgoing was not enough for him; he was also eager to see how much more of a high he could get.

"I was sort of mixing everything together: weed, lots of beer, and Ritalin," he remembers. "There was a short period of time when my ready supply of the Ritalin was cut off, though—Phil got kicked out of school! It wasn't because of the drugs; he'd been fooling around in art class and got sent out in the hall. That was sort of dumb of the teacher—she should have known he couldn't be trusted out there on his own if he couldn't be trusted in the classroom.

"Anyway, Phil took these big tall trash cans and climbed up on them. Then he started pushing in all the ceiling tiles in the hall. So he got kicked out—actually, one of his many suspensions. The bottom line was that, while it was easy to get the pills from Phil at school each day, I couldn't very well go over to his house to stock up.

"Luckily, another friend was diagnosed with the same condition as Phil. His name was Tyler, and he got Ritalin tablets, not the capsules Phil had gotten. And Tyler was more than willing to share. It was different—a more powerful high. I'd drink and maybe do weed. And then I'd chop up those pink tablets and snort them. I was doing about ninety milligrams a day, I think. That's a lot, and I started feeling it right away. I was getting chest pains; it was hurting my heart.

"I really worried for a time that I was going to have a heart attack," admits Joe. "But it didn't really stop me from snorting those pills or drinking at the same time. I was showing up at every party, getting high and drunk. I was out of control—passing out in people's cars, people I didn't even know."

Was it difficult for him, as a fourteen-year-old, to get so much alcohol? Joe laughs.

"Not a bit," he says. "Most people just had it around. Or if they didn't, there were plenty of people I could get to buy it for me. Sometimes if my friends and I were really desperate, we'd just sneak into an older kid's party and tap their keg. No one really noticed. Or if they did, it wasn't a big deal. Remember, this was a small town, and that's what kids did."

MOTOCROSS

Ironically, at the same time that Joe was abusing his body pounding down beer and drugs, he was excelling at his favorite sport.

"It's motocross," he says with a smile. "The best sport in the world. It's racing and riding on these small motorcycles. You do jumps and stuff. Ninth grade, that was the best—it was filled with motocross. I mean, I was good. My ninth grade year I was fifth in the state.

"I haven't talked that much about my stepdad," he adds. "And lots of times we've had problems. But motocross is the one thing we'd always done together. He got me riding when I was really little, back in California. He'd take me to meets every Sunday without fail.

"It's an expensive sport, too. A bike costs around thirty-two hundred dollars. And each weekend, a meet ran about two hundred dollars. Not cheap, no. But my stepdad is a mechanic, so he was real good at fixing the bikes up."

How was he able to race when he was using drugs and alcohol? Joe shakes his head impatiently.

"No, I didn't use on the weekends," he says. "I never mixed the two; I never wanted to. The high from motocross—man, it's like nothing else in the world, better than any drug. I didn't want to have anything interfere with the high from racing. I mean, the jumps—well, it's like flying. Trust me, it's amazing. The speed, the danger—there's nothing like it. It's really a rush. So from Friday to Sunday I wouldn't be using weed, pills, or alcohol."

"My Parents Were Starting to Get Suspicious"

Joe remembers that it was in his sophomore year of high school that his drug and alcohol use was becoming more flagrant.

"My drinking was heavier; I was consuming unbelievable amounts of beer," he says. "And I was using new drugs: crystal meth and crank. I was still using Ritalin, too, but this stuff was better, more intense. Crystal meth was actually cleaner than crank. Crank is sort of a dirty yellow, but the crystal meth is pure white. It had a big sting, a big rush, too. I loved that sting in my nose when I used it. I guess I knew that I would soon be calm, more outgoing. I'd get shivers in my head—that's the only way I can describe it—and a kind of jolt. Then I'd let it die down for a bit; then I'd take another hit. For me the high lasted an hour or more.

"My grades were still terrible. I know that my parents were starting to get suspicious that it wasn't just a phase I was going through; there was something else going on that was interfering with my schoolwork. They knew I'd gotten high a couple of times, I think. I know they knew I drank once in a while. But they had no idea how often it was happening.

"My dad would call me over at Tyler's house; I'd be all drunk or stoned. He'd tell me, 'Say, Joe, you better get home because it's time for dinner.' Well, no way could I pass any kind of a sobriety test! But I respected him enough to go home—I couldn't just stay away. I didn't want to disobey him, you know what I mean? So he'd look at me real funny when I got home. I know he was real disappointed in me, they both were. And he finally told me he didn't want me over at Tyler's house anymore."

State Champ

In 1996 Joe won the state championship for his age bracket in motocross—the proudest moment of his life.

"You gotta notice this jacket," he says, swiveling in his chair to show off the words *1996 State Champ* embroidered on the back. "It's like my most important possession, probably the only thing I'd run into a burning building to save, I guess. So that was a big deal for me.

Joe's drinking caused him to let things slip away—grades, his relationship with his parents, his motocross state championship, and almost his life.

"I was treated real good, too. People wanted to hang out with me, stuff like that. It was golden, being me. People were real impressed with who I was. I never took the jacket off!"

But he also admits that while he had cut down on his drug use, he was getting drunk more than ever before.

"I still didn't like the taste, just like when I was a little kid," he says. "But it was the means to an end. And I loved the end. Not hanging with Tyler, I didn't have access to the Ritalin like before, but the drinking was easy. And yeah, I still kept the balance between weekends and weekdays—kept motocross separate. But getting drunk was taking more and more of my time.

"And what happened was everything just sort of got away from me after that. After being state champion, I kind of let it slip away. It was me, drinking and mixing the drinking with drugs. Things got really bad, and all of a sudden being state champ, and doing the motocross stuff with my stepdad, that all went away."

"I CAN STILL FEEL IT TO THIS DAY"

Things came to a climax for Joe one evening after he had been heavily drinking beer and vodka straight from the bottle.

"Two drinks like that and you're buzzed ten minutes later," says Joe. "I mean, that alone would have been enough to get me as high as I wanted to be. But that same evening I started mixing acid with my liquor.

"See, I was hanging around with this one friend. He and I decided we'd buy some acid; he gave me the money, and I went to get the stuff for both of us. Anyway, I scored the acid like I was supposed to, but when I got back, my friend had been arrested. He'd been on house arrest for something—I'm not sure what he'd done; I don't remember.

"So anyway, I watch him being driven away in the back of the squad car, and I'm thinking, I really don't know what to do with this acid, exactly. I'd had a little crystal meth that day, plus the liquor. So I decided I'd just do both of the hits of acid, his and mine. Plus, I had some Ritalin, so I snorted that at the same time I dropped the acid."

Joe smiles sheepishly at the obvious question.

"I know, I know—why?" he says, holding his hands up. "I know now that it was a lot for my age. I know that all now. I didn't know it then, though. It's like, I just wanted to see how much different, how much higher I could feel."

Joe pushes gently on his chest, remembering. "That got me rushing. I could feel it right in here, in my heart. In fact, I can still feel it to this day, a pain, right in here. I just kept rubbing my chest here, even pounding on it, to make the pain stop. And after a little while, I decided to go out to the High Bridge."

THE HIGH BRIDGE

There is a bridge outside of town, Joe says, a railroad bridge that stretches over 160 feet above the water and is a mile long. Known as the High Bridge, it is a favorite hangout for teenagers.

"On one side of the bridge there's a railing, and the other side is just a dropoff," he explains. "We used to go out there and get drunk sometimes and hold on to the railing when a train went by. It would just shake! The train would go by so close that you could reach out and touch it, too. These were fast-moving trains, too. And it was really strange when you were drunk—it was nuts. The biggest rush—holding on and the bridge was shaking like crazy. Your friends are all lined up next to you, drinking their beer and whatever, and everybody's wasted.

"Anyway, with the combination of the acid, the Ritalin, and the alcohol, I started flipping out. I was seeing stuff I didn't want to see. Like, I saw my friend all drunk walking across the train tracks. He got his leg stuck, and I thought he was going to fall and die or get run over. I just thought, 'Man, I gotta get off this bridge.' So I dragged myself off the High Bridge and drank a forty-ouncer of beer. I got a joint from somewhere, and I started smoking that, too, just to calm down, you know?

"And I met up with my friend, and we walked back to his place for a while, but I was hallucinating so bad I was getting scared. I kept seeing these flashes of light, like stars falling down out of the sky. Anyway, I went off by myself, just to take a walk. It was like three in the morning; my parents thought I was sleeping over at a friend's house, so no one was wondering where I was. And my heart was pounding out of my chest. I was messed up really bad from the drinking, from the drugs.

"I got scared and banged on the door of this one house. I was yelling, 'Call 911! Call 911!' They answered the door, but they slammed it in my face. I thought I was going to die—I really did."

"It Was a Higher Power, I Know That"

Unable to get help from nearby houses, Joe decided to keep walking toward home. Drunk and disoriented, he was surprised to find the basement door unlocked.

"That was strange," he says, shaking his head. "I mean, that door is never open. But I opened it up and found the phone. I just lay down on the floor; I was still hallucinating. I dialed 911 myself, and when the operator answered, I couldn't really say anything. I just said something like, 'I can't get to where my parents are' or something. And then I blacked out.

"Everything went sort of whitish. I went into a coma and stayed that way for seventeen hours. I wasn't aware of it, of course, but afterwards they told me I'd had three epileptic seizures from the combination of the drinking and the drugs. They knew that as soon as they took a blood sample; my parents weren't able to fill them in at all. I mean, I'd never told them what I'd been doing.

"Anyway, the next day I woke up. I had all these attachments on me; I was all connected up. I can remember that all I wanted was to get out of there. That's when this lady came in and talked to me about going to treatment for my drug and alcohol problems. She told me that if I hadn't called 911, I would have died in half an hour."

Joe shakes his head. "I think of that a lot, you know? It's kind of like God helped me, I think. I mean, why would my basement door have been unlocked—then of all times? And why did I have just enough time to dial 911 before I blacked out? It was a higher power, I know that."

"I Felt Cleansed"

Feeling more focused than he had in months, Joe agreed to begin treatment.

"I went to a twenty-one-day program at Cambridge," he says. "I just knew it was the right thing to do after talking to that lady in the hospital. And I took everything very, very seriously in treatment. I was really into it. I had wonderful counselors, and that was great. I liked everyone there. I know it sounds funny maybe, but I mean it—I really liked treatment.

"After the three weeks were up, I felt that I was a very strong person. I was off booze, off drugs, and twenty-one days was a long time for me. To be truthful, I don't think I'd gone that long without a drink or a hit of some drug in years. I felt cleansed, like I was cured completely. And to tell you the honest-to-God truth, I intended more than anything to stay that way."

Joe says that the first thing he did after going home was to tell his friends about what he had accomplished.

"I wanted to talk to them, tell them how cool it was to be sober. I was thinking like, 'Man, this is great! You guys should try this!' That's what I was going to do for those guys. And it was so typical, too—I found them all sitting around a picnic table at the park smoking weed. I sat down with them, and the first time they passed it to me, I said no."

Looking uncomfortable, Joe admits, "The second time, like ten minutes later, I took a hit."

He laughs derisively, as though the memory makes him sick.

"I was so mad at myself," he says quietly. "But, you know, it's funny. I was thinking to myself that all those people back in treatment really liked me. And I liked them. So that was all cool. But now I'm back where I really live, with the friends that I'm going to see every day. And I have to learn to live in their world, you know?

After his brush with death, Joe decided he needed to enter a treatment program.

"Anyway, that's how I told it to myself. I figured I'd just do what they did, and that I'd just have to learn to do things in moderation. I mean, none of those guys had been half an hour away from dying in some hospital. I just needed to take it a little easier, maybe just a beer or a little weed once in a while. I figured I could handle that."

"Back to Cambridge"

But his plan did not work, Joe says. Although he tried to avoid drugs, he was drinking more than he ever had.

"I kind of gave up hard liquor for a while," he says. "It made me feel weird. I'd go outside at a party after having vodka or whatever, and I'd throw up all over and pass out. So I just stuck to beer—didn't get as sick. I was still drinking to get drunk, though. It wasn't enough just to get a little buzzed; I needed more than that.

"I was the funny drunk," he continues. "I was the nice, funny guy at the party. And I'd pass out after drinking a while, and then I'd wake up and be funny all over again. I didn't like to leave parties, so I'd try to be the last one to go. I'd always say, 'I need another beer.' I just had the feeling that I didn't want to miss any of the drinking, you know? If there was a beer that hadn't been opened, I wanted it."

Before long, Joe realized that he needed to go back to Cambridge for treatment.

"My mom drove me back up there," he says. "My stepdad—I guess he was supportive, too, but I'd let him down a lot. The motocross stuff we'd done together had sort of fallen by the wayside. Everybody had heard that I'd been in treatment, so I was the subject of a lot of gossip. I was labeled an alcoholic, a drug addict."

Did those labels fit? Joe shrugs.

"I guess so," he says. "But it made me feel bad that motocross had gotten all screwed up. I had tried to keep my two lives separate, you know? I didn't want motocross to be ruined. But it was, and my relationship with my stepdad sort of got ruined, too."

Trying to Stay Sober

Over the next year Joe tried treatment two more times. Each time, he says, he was successful a little longer than the time before; however, he always relapsed.

"I still loved treatment," he says. "I'd get a good relationship going with my counselor and my group, and then I'd go home and things would be OK for a while. And then down I'd go, drinking again.

"The third time I went to a different kind of treatment—it was a halfway house. I was there three months. I loved it! There were five girls and fifteen guys, and we lived in this house. We had limits; we had stuff we had to do each day. We cooked, we cleaned. It was great, except that they had this no-contact rule there; they didn't want us breaking down into little cliques. They wanted everyone to be one solid group, I guess you could say.

"I ended up getting pretty serious about this one girl, Angie. I really liked her a lot, so the no-contact rule was tough for me. One night we were all up north camping—with the counselors and everything—and I wanted to spend some time alone just talking to Angie. So I just said, 'The hell with it—I'm going to talk to whoever I want to.' So I did, and I got kicked out."

Joe says that he was devastated; he did not want to leave.

"I was crying; I was really emotional," he says bluntly. "It was the nicest place I'd ever been. But I had to leave and so I did. I went home and decided that the only way I was going to stay sober was to stay in the house, just avoid my friends and all that temptation!

"It was so hard. I'd see my friends driving up and down the road, and I wanted to be with them, you know? I still had lots of cravings to drink, too. When I got those cravings, I'd turn on the TV or something or maybe eat. Another thing I did was I started lifting weights. That helped, too.

"After about a month of being home, my grandma told me I could rent out the basement of her place in the city. That's how I got here. I had a job in the factory where my mom works, making stuff for circuit boards. And so I was making like seven dollars an hour. I had a car, drove to work, went to AA meetings all the time, like they'd told us to do at treatment. And I was away from the temptations of that little town—things seemed OK."

"I KNEW I WAS GOING TO DRINK"

Joe says that he started slipping a little almost right away.

"I wasn't drinking or anything," he says. "But I started skipping AA meetings. I was so tired, you know, after working all day. I'd think, well, I was working hard, and I wasn't drinking or using drugs. I just wanted to relax and that should be OK.

When Joe decided to call an old friend, he knew he was really making the decision to relapse.

"Then I started thinking I'd go out with some of my friends from the halfway house. I hadn't seen them in a while, and a few of them lived in the city, too. So I'd make time to do that. Looking back, maybe I should have done the meetings more often, I don't know."

He rubs his hands over his face. "Everything really fell apart one night when I got a call from Phil, the guy from my hometown. I don't really know how he got in touch with me. It was kind of nice hearing from him, so we talked. And then one night I called him up. I wanted some fun, some action. I was tired of the life I had, I guess you could say, tired of the same old same old.

"I'll tell you something else—I knew I was going to drink, too. I knew that when I was calling Phil; what I was really deciding was that I was going to relapse. Anyway, his sister knew the owners of this one club, so even though we weren't eighteen, we could get in. I got in my car and picked him up, and we were off.

"Right away when we walked into the club, I got a drink—some weird greenish-looking thing. I still don't know what it was, but it tasted like really sweet Kool-Aid or something. I had another one, and another one, and another one. And then we had someone buy us a case of Budweiser, twenty-four in the case. And that was me, getting really drunk, after five months of being sober."

A Car Chase

Joe's evening did not end there, unfortunately. He decided that what he really wanted to do was go driving, so he found two willing passengers, Matt and Kelly.

"That was so bad, such a bad mistake," he says. "I'll tell you, somebody else just took over my body; I was like a monster. I was driving 100, 105 miles an hour. I don't know, something just took hold of me. I remember swerving, thinking I was going to hit a deer, but I stayed on the road. By all rights, we should have been killed, and it would have been all my fault.

"I remember heading into this town called Chisago. I'd be driving along so fast, and I'd just lose track of the road. All of a sudden a curb would come up, and I'd be speeding along on grass, you know? I'm like, what the hell? And the girl, Kelly, she was yelling, 'Stop the car, stop the car!' I'd think I was so clever. I'd stop at the stoplight, and then I'd burn rubber—I'd get out of there before she could get out. 'Too late,' I'd say.

"I was on Highway 8; it's a bad rural highway. Lots of people have gotten in accidents on it. But I'm booking; I've never seen my speedometer go so high. And Kelly and Matt are yelling at me, but I'm saying, 'Hey, don't worry, I've done this lots of times.'

"I saw all these cars coming up, their taillights. I was coming up behind them so fast. I decided to pass them, only there's some on-coming cars, so I swerve into a ditch. And then Matt starts yelling to me that the car I almost hit was a state trooper. He's like, 'Man, you gotta stop—that was a cop!'"

"What Did I Do?"

Joe did not want to stop, however, and the police followed him in a high-speed chase down the dark highway.

"Kelly kept screaming, 'They're going to catch us; throw the beer out the window!' and she was tossing cans of beer out the back. I remember being so angry that she was throwing beer away that I stopped watching the road. I was yelling to her, 'You throw one more beer out, and I'm going to be pissed as hell.' That was all I cared about.

"Anyway, that's when I lost control of the car. We went into a ditch; I blew a tire going about ninety miles an hour, and the police came up to the car. Man, that was so scary! They're yelling, 'Driver! Get your hands on top of your head!' I had guns trained on me; I was thinking, man, I could die here. I did everything they told me to do. They handcuffed me and took me to jail. Matt and Kelly got taken someplace so they could call their parents, I think."

Joe says that the incident frightened him more than anything else.

"After I went to jail, they took me to the hospital for blood tests. I was .12—way up there. Then I went to detox. It isn't really like anything—you just stay there, feeling like shit. They take away all your clothes, give you a little robe and some orange juice. And it hits me—I'm wandering around in this robe, drinking this stuff, and I'm like, 'Wow, what did I do?'

"I kept thinking how not only did I relapse, but I almost killed myself as well as other people, too. I worried about how my parents were going to take it when the cops told them. I would lose my job because I lost my car. I was just panicking. I was seventeen at that point and a minor, and I was being charged with a felony—fleeing from an officer. Plus, they gave me two DWIs [driving while intoxicated]. I'm actually still waiting to go to trial for that."

Trying to Change

After being released from detox, Joe knew he had to do something to turn his life around. Going back to AA seemed like the best first step.

"I went to thirty meetings in thirty days," he says proudly. "I kept my momentum going pretty good. I don't know how, but I did it. Dave, my AA sponsor, had a spare room that he was going to be renting out in a week or two but said I could stay there until I found my own place. I got a job, too, being a stockboy at a grocery store. So things were OK for a while.

"But one night I ended up staying overnight at a friend's house. He was a guy I'd known from the halfway house; he was in AA, too. Anyway, I came back the next day, back to Dave's house, and he'd written me a note. He told me that he removed my stuff, and I should leave my key under the door. See, Dave thought I'd been out drinking. I hadn't, and that made me so mad. I didn't want to see him ever again; he didn't even talk to me about it, never even gave me a chance to explain. He probably wouldn't have believed me anyway, I guess.

"So I stopped going to AA. I figured, who cares? They just think the worst of you anyway. And I'd worked so hard, going to all those meetings. It still makes me mad, thinking about it."

"I'VE SCREWED UP TOO MANY TIMES"

Joe felt that he could not face his family again. He had heard about a shelter for teens, and he walked there to ask for help.

"I hadn't relapsed," he says. "I just needed somewhere to live, and everything was so complicated. They helped me out at the

Although Joe has managed to get into a residential treatment program, he has started smoking and drinking again, actions that could get him kicked out.

shelter and got me on the waiting list for a transitional living place called Archdale. I stayed at the shelter for two months while waiting for space to open up at Archdale. I kept working, too, still being a stockboy."

Joe looks uncomfortable. He says it is very hard talking about the times he has failed.

"I'd like to say that things were fine, but they're not," he admits. "See, I got into Archdale, and everything should have been OK. But I started smoking weed and drinking a couple nights after I got in. I know that was stupid. I tell myself that all the time.

"The people there gave me chances. And I'm worried because of this trial coming up; the judge had told me that if I get kicked out of my transitional living arrangement, I could go to jail. I'm supposed to have a meeting with the counselor at Archdale today at two o'clock. I don't know what's going to happen. Keith could decide to kick me out; I don't know if I even deserve another chance.

"I still talk to my mom sometimes on the phone. She's great. My stepdad's still mad at me, and I can understand that. He told me that once I turned eighteen, he never wanted me back home again."

Joe sighs and puts his head down in his arms. "I've screwed up too many times," he says, more to himself than to anyone else.

Miranda

"I MEAN I'D BEEN DRINKING AND SMOKING WEED BEFORE I WAS IN SEVENTH GRADE EVEN. BUT I'LL TELL YOU, USING WAS A BIG PART OF MY LIFE THEN. IT MADE SPENDING TIME AWAY FROM HOME A LOT MORE ENJOYABLE. BUT I NEVER HAD ANY IDEA THAT I'D BE CALLING MYSELF AN ALCOHOLIC BY THE TIME I WAS SIXTEEN."

Author's Note: Miranda is an attractive sixteen-year-old who has chosen to attend Sobriety High. She is, by her own admission, an alcoholic who has always run away from things. Her long history of running away from home is a case in point. She is very social and is well liked by almost everyone at her school. She is uncertain about her own future, even about whether she will ever drink again. The embarrassing consequences of her drunkenness are her motivation for staying sober now.

Miranda is not in her usual affable mood.

"I'm so mad," she fumes, throwing a notebook into her locker. "I can't figure out why I keep losing my cigarettes. And I need to smoke for a few minutes before we talk, you know?"

She brushes back a lock of jet black hair from her eyes and jams her hand into her coat pocket.

"Aha! Here they are!" she cries, holding a crumpled pack of cigarettes triumphantly above her head. "OK, just give me a minute, OK?"

She runs outside, joining the student body in what appears to be a popular ritual at the end of the school day.

"It's Not All That Unusual"

Five minutes later Miranda has returned. She smiles and sinks into a sofa.

"I shouldn't smoke, I know that," she confides. "But I've had to give up weed, alcohol; I guess this is my last vice."

Miranda is an admitted alcoholic. She shakes her head when asked if sixteen is awfully young to know something like that about herself.

"It's not all that unusual, really," she says. "I've been in treatment, and I've gotten to know kids that are lots younger than that—twelve, thirteen. That's a stereotype that people have, that alcoholics are bums, or men, or older, or something. I know there are plenty of old men who are drinkers out there, but there are alcoholics of all types: women, girls, boys.

"Myself, I started drinking at a real young age, and it got the better of me. That's the best way I can say it. I got to the point where the consequences of drinking were bad—way too bad. I was with the wrong crowd, and I knew it. I was over the edge, yeah."

Adopted

Miranda knows that her home life has contributed to the problems she has had with alcohol and drugs, although neither substance was used by other members of her family.

"I was adopted when I was two months old," she explains. "I was born in India—you can probably tell that. My birth mother brought me to the orphanage when I was really little, and there was already a family waiting for me in the United States. Calcutta, where I was born, is a really poor city. Baby girls aren't valued much; probably no babies are valued very much, I guess. So I was lucky to come to this country.

"When my mom—my adopted mom—and her husband had applied to adopt me, they were really wanting to get a divorce. But my mom really wanted me, and back then it was a rule that you had to be married to adopt. So they stayed together a little while longer. Soon after I came, they divorced. My mom's name is Helen; she's the one who raised me.

"I have to be honest and to say that my mom and I have not gotten along very well," Miranda says, looking down. "In fact, it's just been in the last year that we've gotten to the point where we can get along on a regular basis. I can actually say that I think of her as my mother now, where before I really didn't."

Miranda blames a bad relationship with her mother (seated across from Miranda) for some of her problems with drugs and alcohol.

"ALWAYS A SOCIAL GIRL"

Her memories of herself as a young girl are pleasant, she says.

"My mom has other kids, too," she says. "I've got three sisters and one brother, and growing up was fun, at least for a while. My mom worked; she still does. She's a social worker for the county. She works with people on welfare and stuff like that. And on the weekends she works at a twenty-four-hour grocery store, just for extra money. I'll say this about my mom—she's always been an incredibly hard worker. And with so many kids to take care of, the money was really needed.

"I loved playing outside when I was little," she says. "I loved makeup and hair and looking at fashion magazines, too. I guess I was pretty typical of a lot of kids. But the thing I remember most is that I always had friends around. I loved being with other people. That would get me in trouble when I was young, like at school. I was the one talking and whispering and giggling, you know? I didn't mean it in a bad way, and the teachers never really were angry with me. But it was like, 'Miranda, sit down,' or 'Miranda, no whispering, please.' I was always a social girl."

Miranda says that she and her mother argued occasionally when she was younger, but their arguments were almost always resolved.

"I'd want to stay out later than she was willing to let me," she says. "Or maybe I'd want to go over to a friend's house, but my mom wanted me to stay home. Things like that were little problems. But they got bigger as I got older. It seemed like when I got older, me and my mom couldn't agree on anything."

RUNNING AWAY

It was at this time that Miranda began a pattern of running away that was to continue over the next several years.

"It was a big thing with me," she says, smiling. "Eleven or twelve, that's when it started. In a way, I think that my running away was what started everything else that was bad in my life—taking drugs, drinking way too much and too often. It was how I decided to handle problems at home. If my mom yelled at me, or if I was mad about something, I'd pack a bag and go to my friend's house.

"At first it was only once in a while; I'd be gone for a few hours or so. But as time went on—especially when I got to be like thirteen or fourteen—it was all the time. I mean it! I really was as addicted to running away as I was later to alcohol.

"But later, I'd run a lot. It was mostly because of the fights my mom and I had. See, our fights were lots more serious than before. Not that they were about anything really serious—it was the same kind of disagreements we'd had when I was young. Only now, it seemed like she got a lot madder. Things really escalated, you could say."

Miranda shrugs. "Abuse, yeah, that was part of it. Not just spankings, no; it was way worse than that. She'd hit me. And when she did that, I'd react. I have to be honest and say that it was partly me, too. I'd hit her back, and I really regret that now. I never punched her, no, but I'd push her away or scratch her. It was usually just to get her off me. But it was wrong, and I feel bad about that looking back.

"So anyway, the fight would end with me reacting. And then it would be like, 'Screw you—I'll just leave.' So that's what I did. And because I was really angry with my mom, I'd stay gone longer than just a few hours. Sometimes it was days, or even weeks as I got older."

THE BLACK SHEEP

Her siblings had the same complaints—fights with their mother—but Miranda did not feel that they were treated as badly as she was.

"That was one thing, too," she explains. "I mean, here I am, the adopted one; they're all her biological children. And she's slapping me, hitting me. Maybe she yells at them, but it isn't the same. And plus, she's saying really hurtful things—hardcore emotional abuse, I think. Stuff you should never say to a child, like, 'I don't love you,' or 'I don't care about you,' or 'Why did we ever adopt you?'"

Miranda says that the constant fighting seemed to drive a wedge between her and her family.

"I'm thinking, 'OK, I'm the adopted one, and I'm being told that she doesn't love me.' So it didn't take me too long to figure out that something was wrong. Oh, gosh, I can't tell you how much I felt like an outcast, like the real black sheep. Not just the color thing—that was a huge thing with me, too, having an all-white family, being around white people all the time—but being differ-ent, being unloved."

Asked why she thinks her mother was so angry, Miranda shrugs.

"I've thought about that a lot," she admits. "And I haven't fig-ured out why; I don't know. I think my mom had a really hard childhood and that she's got a lot of things wrong with her that she hasn't dealt with herself. Maybe that's why she takes it out on her kids, and me in particular. But that's just a guess."

LOOKING FOR MIRANDA

Miranda says she got a little support from her older siblings, but it was usually not enough.

"They were all older than me," she says. "I mean, Angie is the closest in age to me, and she's four years older. So when I was thir-teen or so, she's seventeen—off working or being with her friends. A lot of the time no one was home but my mom and me.

"There were a few times when my brother Tom would try to split us up. He'd tell us to stop the yelling, and we would, at least for a while. But there were also a lot of times when my brother and sisters would just turn their heads and let us figure it out.

"The result was me leaving. It got to the point where my friends weren't surprised at all to see me show up on their doorstep. And almost always they'd be good about letting me stay. Even most of their parents would be supportive; they'd cover for me. They'd say, 'You're not going home; you stay here,' and I would. A lot of those people were really easygoing."

Miranda says that her family spent a lot of time searching for her.

"They had phone numbers of all my friends, even friends they'd never met," she explains. "The whole family would look for me. I still have a poster on my wall in my room that my brother posted one time. It has a picture of me with the word RUNAWAY under it. It says, If You See Me, Call This Number—it was the police. That was a time when I was gone for three weeks. I think the longest was almost a month."

How was she able to avoid her family for that long? She smiles.

"A lot of the time, all my friends would know where I was. And if my brother or anyone else went to one of their houses, they'd call the house I was staying at. They'd say, 'Miranda, your van just left our house.' So then I knew I had to leave, because they were getting close. Maybe I'd go to a house they'd already been to—it just depended."

SKIPPING SCHOOL

While she was on the run, Miranda almost always skipped school, too.

"I knew that was one of the first places they would look," she says. "So I'd stay away from school. And seventh and eighth grades, those were bad times for me as a student. All the missed classes caught up with me eventually, too. I was so far behind that I failed eighth grade. Yeah, I should be a junior in high school now, not a sophomore.

"It isn't that I'm a bad student," she maintains. "I'm not dumb or anything. It's just that I never did the work back then. I never took tests, never did the projects or the reports. And when I was in school, I wasted my time. I started getting a bad attitude, and using my mouth more than I should. I'd get suspensions, and that would be even more missed school! That was completely my fault—nobody else's.

"The boring part was being on the run when my friends were in school," she says. "They'd give me their keys, so I could stay in their houses while they were at school. Their parents would be working, so I'd have the house to myself. I'd watch television, just sit around. I stayed inside most of the time; I knew if I went shopping or something, there was more chance that I'd get stopped for being truant."

Using Alcohol

During this part of her life, Miranda says, she was using a great deal of drugs and alcohol.

"It didn't start then," she explains. "I mean I'd been drinking and smoking weed before I was in seventh grade even. But I'll tell you, using was a big part of my life then. It made spending time away from home a lot more enjoyable. But I never had any idea that I'd be calling myself an alcoholic by the time I was sixteen.

When Miranda ran away from home, she skipped school, her grades suffered, and she eventually got suspended.

"The first time I drank was at my friend Mike's house. I was over there one Friday night, and we figured we'd give it a try. His dad had some beer around, so we drank that; I had one and a half beers. I don't know; it just seemed like a cool thing to try.

"I remember that we got really drunk, and I loved it! I loved the feeling of being drunk—it wasn't the taste or anything that I liked. Anyway, I drank a couple times more after that, on and off. And by the time I was in seventh grade, I was drinking a lot. It was every weekend for sure and once or twice during the school week."

Miranda says that she had no opportunity to get liquor from her own house.

"No one in my family was a drinker," she says, "so I couldn't get any from home. But it was easy to get it other places. I mean, Mike could get it or older friends. Sometimes my friends who had parents who drank could sneak vodka. You know, that old trick where you find the vodka bottle under the sink, empty some out, and fill the bottle with water? So we did that sometimes. I don't remember that getting liquor was ever much of a problem, even at that age."

Using Weed

Because she was used to the feeling of being drunk, Miranda says that it was not much of a step from alcohol to marijuana.

"I'd been holding out for a while," she confides. "I knew that a lot of my friends had been smoking weed for a month or two the summer before seventh grade. I just didn't think I wanted to get into it, I guess. But one night at my friend Ryan's party, I just decided to try.

"One of my friends asked me, and I said OK. So we went to the back of the house and smoked like three bowls of weed. And I loved it—absolutely loved it! I didn't get high, but I loved the taste, I loved the idea of it."

"The idea of it"? Miranda shrugs and smiles.

"I mean, the whole thing of sitting around with your friends, being with people you like, talking—that's what I loved. It seemed like it wasn't bad. I mean, anything that could get people together to have a good time, to be happy, was a good thing. Anyway, that's what I thought then.

"And so me and my friends, we started doing it more often, usually on a daily basis. We had no trouble finding it, not really. I mean, there were always plenty of people we knew who sold it. The only little problem was money. I didn't have a job; we were all too young to do anything except maybe baby-sitting. To have enough to smoke, we needed at least twenty dollars—to make it worthwhile, you know? Well, some of the kids would sell stuff, like pawn it, jewelry or whatever. I never did that, though. What I would do is steal from my family."

"It Was Easy to Take Their Money"

Miranda looks down at her hands folded in her lap.

"I'm not proud of that, you know. I didn't feel bad about it then, while I was doing it. Back then I hated my family a lot of the time, so it was easy to take their money. I mean, Angie and Tom were nice to me sometimes, but I still felt like my mom treated them better than me. And I resented that, yeah. So when I thought about it in those terms, well, I didn't have much problem with stealing from them.

"I did a few other drugs, too," she says. "For a few months I was using prescription drugs—uppers and downers, mostly. And I'd take them with alcohol, which is about the worst thing you can do. But I still liked drinking—as much, if not more than, using drugs. And I liked the hallucinations I'd get when I mixed the two. I tried cocaine a little bit and some 'shrooms, but that's all."

Miranda remembers that some of her friends' parents would use drugs, too, or provide them to the young people.

"That was weird," she says, shaking her head. "Even I recognized how weird that was back then. It was like some of these parents hadn't gotten beyond their teenage mentality; they liked to party with us. I mean, to get high with your friend's mom? But I guess I must have gotten past that because I did get high a lot.

"They often supplied us with liquor, too, and for the same reasons. I mean, we were young, like thirteen or fourteen. We'd give them money sometimes, or sometimes they'd just buy it. And they'd get us wine coolers, beer, and even hard liquor. But to blame them for being irresponsible is only part of it, I know. Like I said, no one forced us to smoke weed or to drink. We have to accept our share of the blame."

"I Got a Nice Little Buzz"

Miranda says that even though her friends were aware of how much she was getting drunk or high, adults in her life had no idea.

"My mom didn't know," she says flatly. "I mean, I came home blasted many times. Maybe she noticed, but she never said anything. Of course, I tried to avoid coming home if I was really drunk; I didn't want her to catch on if I could help it. I'd usually call her and tell her I was staying over at a friend's. And, of course, if I was running at the time, I didn't worry about a thing. She's seen me high, too, although she didn't put two and two together. She did say, 'Why are your eyes so red?' but I'd just tell her I was really tired. Yeah, red eyes is one of the things that happens when you smoke a lot of weed. Anyway, she bought my explanation, so it must have worked.

"I used both in school, also. I remember smoking weed at the bus stop, in the bathrooms at school, even on the bus! I never got caught; it just wasn't that big a deal. And I'd drink at school. Me and my friends would walk around the halls in the morning drinking screwdrivers [vodka and orange juice]. You'd just put it in a Sunny D bottle, you know, and it just looks like you're drinking orange juice. Or sometimes we'd put Captain Morgan [rum] in with some Pepsi in the Pepsi bottle. We'd carry alcohol with us in the morning, have it in our backpacks.

"I never got really plastered, really drunk at school," she maintains. "I mean, what would be the point? If I'd done that, I would have given myself away, or I'd have done something crazy at school to call attention to myself. I didn't want to get in trouble. This way, being kind of secretive, I got a nice little buzz and went to class.

"There were times, though, when we'd have to act sober, like if we were partying and we were going to someone's house and might see their parents. What we'd usually do is smoke like a million cigarettes to get rid of the alcohol smell. Or we'd eat a lot, which wasn't too smart because we'd puke. Or drink milk—that takes the smell off your breath, too."

"I Didn't Need It"

Miranda stresses that she never physically felt an overwhelming need for a drink, as some alcoholics do.

"I didn't need it; I liked it," she says. "The addiction wasn't as much a physical craving, like 'I can't get through a day without it.' I have a problem with alcohol; I'm an alcoholic. I'm addicted to the process, the wanting to drink and have fun. And because of the alcohol involved in that, it became a problem."

Miranda says she didn't crave alcohol; she says she drank to fit in with her friends.

Although she still cares a great deal for the friends she had then, Miranda firmly believes that her drinking and using drugs were all wrapped up in her peer group.

"It was just the way we were," she shrugs. "I don't think they are bad people at all—they're my friends. We were all loyal to one another; when someone was in trouble, we stuck by them. But in that peer group, drinking—especially drinking—was very important. Drinking with those guys was something I just didn't question. That's how we related to each other. Beer was as casual to us as drinking pop. That's really what it was like.

"Just like the very first time I smoked weed—that was what drinking in our group was like. I loved the camaraderie, the kicking back and having fun. I loved the nonthreatening atmosphere, the relaxing. I was addicted to that sort of fun, where the drinking interfered with everything. But the consequences just got worse and worse. It got to a point where drinking and doing that stuff just wasn't worth the consequences."

"Once I Got Drunk, Something Happened"

Miranda explains that when she drank to excess, her judgment was poor. There were many times when, after she had sobered up, she was ashamed of herself.

"I got trashed; I did stupid things," she says. "Simple as that. I was a bad person when I drank. Like I said, I liked the feeling and the mood and everything while it was happening. But once I got drunk, something happened. That's what I mean by *consequences.* My moods were really crazy. If I had the slightest, slightest bad mood before I drank, I'd just start crying uncontrollably once I drank. That happened to me several times, where I'd just ruin the whole evening; I couldn't control my mood. I'd get depressed like that, and other people around me would get depressed, too.

"Other times I'd get violent. I never really went out and beat people up, but I did the next worse thing. I was very, very mean to my friends, or I'd say things to hurt them, knowing it was really wrong. That was strange because at the time I said it, I knew it was hurtful. But because of the drinking, I didn't care. It wasn't that I didn't remember what I said or anything. Your judgment gets so bad—at least mine did—that I knew I was doing wrong, but I didn't care one way or the other."

Drinking Games

Sometimes, Miranda says, she would overreact in ways that would startle both her and her friends.

"Like, we'd be sitting at a friend's house, playing a game. They'd be goofing around, maybe cheat a little. And I'd, like, take my hand and sweep the cards or whatever off the table. I'd yell, 'What do you think you're doing?' Or I'd walk up to one of them and smack them in the back of the head with my hand and tell them how stupid they are.

"You see what I mean?" she asks. "This is what I mean. Consequences like that. I'm not proud of these things; they're embarrassing to remember. The alcohol, the drinking, was bad for me without even ruining my health. It was hurting me personally, emotionally. It was bad; it was making me somebody I wasn't.

"But at the time I couldn't see that. The good—parties, fun— seemed to outweigh anything else. One of the things I liked most to do when I drank was play drinking games. I don't know who made these games up; you'd just learn them, you know? You'd be at a party and someone would say, 'Hey, you guys want to play Temple of Doom, or Presidents and Assholes?'

"Presidents and Assholes was fun. There isn't much of a plot or anything. You go around in a circle and whoever has the highest card is president; the second highest is vice president; the third is someone neutral, and the last one is the asshole. The president can order anyone to drink, for any reason. Like, he could say, 'You have a blue shirt on, so you have to drink.' And that person would drink. And the vice president could tell everyone to drink except

Although Miranda knew that her drinking was wrong, she didn't stop because the alcohol clouded her judgment.

the president. Like that. The poor guy who was the asshole—you can't tell anyone else to drink, but you're always getting told that you have to. You get superplastered," she says.

"Temple of Doom is another one; that was my favorite. You just put cards up, and you have to predict whether the card is going to be red or black. If you are right, you get to make someone else drink; otherwise, you have to take a drink yourself."

Miranda smiles. "It's just games like that, things you do for fun when you're drinking. You can pretty much make any game a drinking game, I guess. But that was my favorite thing to do; when I was at a party and someone had a new game, I'd be like, 'Teach me, teach me!'"

"HELL JUST BROKE LOOSE FOR ME"

It was a strange sort of life, she smiles ruefully, looking back on it—her close bond with her friends and the ever-widening gap between her and her family. Sometimes there would appear to be a truce with her mother, but then things would snap and Miranda would be on the run again.

Miranda once ran away with her boyfriend Nick (pictured), whose mother called the police.

"My mom was getting sick of it," she says. "And the summer before last, when I was fifteen, hell just broke loose for me. I'd been drinking all summer, partying with my friends. I hadn't been home much at all that summer; I think in three months I was home like fourteen days.

"My mom had basically given up, I think. She never knew when I was leaving. Lots of times I'd wait until the middle of the night, or I'd wait a couple of days after a fight. I'd tell her things were OK, and to her it seemed like things were all settled. Then she'd kind of relent, tell me it was OK for me to go out, and then I'd take off. She'd never seen me packing. Tom and my sisters still went out looking for me, but even they were getting tired of it.

"Anyway, this one time I was on the run—it was September 10, I remember that. I'd been going out with this boy Nick—I'm going with him still. I was at his house that day, and he said to me, 'I'm not going to let you go alone; I'm going with you.' Nick and his mom got in a big fight about that. She didn't want him running away, obviously.

"But he just told his mom that he was leaving with me. Nick's mom is great; she's not the kind of mom to call the cops on her own son, but that time she did. Nick and I had just gotten around the corner of the house, and a cop pulls up and asks me, 'Are you Miranda?' I'm like, 'Yeah.' So he told me to come with him. Nick went home. And then everything sort of fell apart."

"A Cold, Dark Room—Just Like a Cell"

The police officer brought Miranda home. Her mother was not happy to have her back, she says.

"She told the cop, 'I can't deal with this anymore; I can't stand her running away all the time.' I was just doing it too often, see. So the cop was like, 'OK, we'll try to find a place for her until things are worked out.' My mom told him I could spend the night at home, and that's it; the next day she wanted me somewhere else.

"I guess it was the cops who suggested that she take me to the hospital the next day. Anyway, the next morning we got in the car and she took me. It was on the sixth floor of the hospital, the chemical dependency unit. My mom had called, and this was suggested as the best place to start. My mom didn't really know that I was drinking so much or taking drugs; she figured I was experimenting, like many kids do, but this hospital was a starting place, I guess."

Miranda says that she absolutely hated it; her one-week stay was the longest week of her life.

"It was like a jail," she says with a shudder. "There were so many rules, you couldn't believe it. I just kept thinking that I hated my mom more than I ever hated her—just for taking me there. To start with, the staff takes all your stuff away from you and does a complete body search. They want to make sure you don't have any drugs or weapons or anything on you. You get put into a cold, dark room—just like a cell. Hard beds, nasty food. You have to ask permission to go to the bathroom or to leave your room for any reason. You knock on the door and the staff person comes and lets you out.

"No belts, no shoelaces—just like if you were in prison," she says. "You just lie on the bed and write—there's nothing else to do. You can't even use a pen because I guess kids have taken pens apart and use the metal part for a weapon. The night I went there—the very first night—a whole bunch of kids tried an attack on the staff. I was trying to get to sleep, you know, and I was having trouble because it was my first night. And all of a sudden I'm hearing this yelling outside. There were some crazy, crazy kids there."

LYING

Asked if she benefited from her stay, Miranda shakes her head emphatically.

"I was sitting there with crazy people, not feeling as though I had anything at all in common with them, not at all. My mom came once and saw me. And after the week was over, I got moved to outpatient. You go there from eight in the morning until four in the afternoon, working on problems. You talk about drugs and drinking, and you do school-type stuff for two or three hours, too. And I hated that, too. I mean, I was using alcohol at that time, but I'd lie and say I wasn't. There was no way they could check, so what did I care?

"After a little while of that, I started running away again. I didn't care anymore. I was tired of being locked up during the day, tired of counselors asking me questions, sick of my mom, sick of everybody telling me what to do. It was just all bullshit for me—that's the best way I can explain how I felt. And my mom could tell things weren't working out; I could tell she was thinking, 'Here we go again.' And she was right—things got worse right after that. I got really drunk on Halloween with my friends; my sister found me and took me back to the hospital. That time is very blurry to me; I can't really remember anything that happened except that I stayed for two weeks this time."

NORD HOUSE

After the end of her second week at the hospital, Miranda was told by the staff that she was going home for the weekend.

"That was a big deal to me, believe it or not," she says. "I'd been confined so long, it seemed like I was never going to be out. Anyway, they told me that the next week I was going to a place called Nord House. I'd heard of it; it has a really great reputation. It's open—a living situation for kids who've had substance abuse problems.

"Anyway, that weekend I could have run. I mean, no one was monitoring me or anything. And I think normally I would have, but just the fact that they were trusting me, and that I was going to this Nord House, that made me want to stay home.

"I liked it right away. There were like five girls living there—just a little house, no different from any other little house. I mean, there was no big sign that told what it was, you know? You go to outpatient stuff, like counseling and stuff, during the day, but instead of going home to the same old problems or whatever, you live there. I thought, 'OK, maybe I can handle this.'

"I was there a month," she says. "And it really turned me around. It wasn't any one person or any one experience. I mean, the staff was great, the other girls were great. And at fifteen, I sure wasn't the youngest—that sort of surprised me. There was a thirteen-year-old there and a fourteen-year-old. We got real close, opened up about some of the things that had made us use alcohol like we had. The counselors were understanding, and they really had great senses of humor. They really cared; it didn't seem like it was just a job for them, like the staff at some other places."

Miranda says that she has thought a lot about why Nord House worked for her when her first treatment experience did not.

"I felt like I wasn't being treated like a prisoner," she says. "I didn't feel like I'd committed a crime. When I was at inpatient, I felt like scum, like a murderer. I'd had bad judgment but nothing worse than that. It was like the punishment was way worse than the crime. So I just didn't feel like listening to whatever they had to say. I mean, it could have been the wisest advice in the world, but I wasn't ready to listen, not then."

CHANGES

Miranda began attending Alcoholics Anonymous meetings while at Nord House and decided she was serious about remaining sober.

"It's a big adjustment," she admits. "A lot of things had to change, mostly about myself. I worried that if I went back home I'd slide back in with the same friends and do the same behaviors that got me in trouble in the first place. I worried about going back to my high school, too. I'd been hanging with the wrong crowd, and they were my friends. What was I supposed to do when I went back? Ignore them?

"The staff at Nord House suggested I look into Sobriety High. It seemed like the best answer for me. I started here a year ago last November, so it's been a while. And they have real strict rules, like you've got to go to AA meetings, and you have to be honest. Those kinds of rules are tougher than you might think!

"I've had one relapse," she admits. "It happened about a month after I started at Sobriety High. It was December 22, right at the beginning of Christmas vacation. I'd been sober since Halloween—that was the time I'd gotten so drunk and my sister took me to the hospital. Well, I went out with the wrong friends. I got really drunk and stripped for some of my guy friends. I don't remember it at all because I had blacked out. One of my girlfriends was worried about me then because I was acting like such a fool."

Miranda looks mortified. "It's embarrassing even now, talking about it, even thinking about it. So she called my mom and told her. I was going to hide the whole thing from my mom, not tell her that I'd been drinking. I guess my plan was to go back to school like nothing had happened, just chalk it up to a mistake.

"But my mom had gotten the phone call, so she knew. She said, 'Miranda, what did you do? You better tell me; you're already busted.' So I confessed everything. I called Judy, the program director at Sobriety High, and told her what I'd done. Well, the consequences could have been really bad, but I got a second chance. I got into a relapse group here at school, and I've worked it out a little bit—going to more AA meetings and that kind of thing. It's a slow process, I'm told, but I'm working at it."

Some Things Don't Change

Interestingly, Miranda has found that she does not hang out with many of the kids from school. Instead, she has gravitated back to her old friends. Does she worry that she will relapse again?

"Not really," she says. "And it isn't like I don't like the kids at Sobriety; I do. I mean, there's a lot we have in common. But I can't give up my old friends. I'm that kind of person that values friendship; if you're a friend of mine, I want to do things with you all the time, you know? So I still see a lot of my old friends.

"But that doesn't mean that I'm back doing the same things with them that I used to," she insists. "I don't. They don't smoke weed or drink in front of me. They have respect for what I'm doing. Most of the time, when they come to see me they know enough to be sober. I know there've been a few occasions when they'll go outside and drink, but I'm OK with that. I can handle it right now because I need to be sober; that's a priority for me at this point in my life."

Looking Ahead

It is difficult to think too far ahead, Miranda says. Nick is her steady boyfriend and has been very supportive. She would like to think that there is a future with him someday.

"He used to be a big drinker, back when I was," she says. "In fact, that's how we met. We were at a party and were both really drunk. We started talking, and he actually ended up dating one of my other friends first. Then after a while the two of us started dating.

"Nick isn't a drinker so much anymore. He's three years older than I am, so he's been around it more than I have. I mean, he does drink, like every once in a while, when he's out with his own friends—which is fine, he can do that. But he doesn't drink around me anymore. He's supportive of me being sober; of everyone I know, Nick is the most supportive.

"We spend like all our time together; it's like we're married. I go to his house every day after school and we hang out. I get home real late, but that's OK with my mom now. She understands what's going on. And his mom is really cool—it's like I'm her daughter."

Miranda says that of all the things that have changed in the past year, her relationship with her mother has meant the most to her.

"We get along a lot better now," she says. "I mean, things aren't perfect, but they aren't in any family. We talk now, which we didn't do before. And she respects me for what I've been through.

"There are a lot of things that she used to say to me that hurt me. But I also know that I drove her to that point a lot. I'm not saying I deserved everything I got; a lot of it was harsh, I thought. But I know I was a real bitch, excuse the language."

Is she done with drinking forever? Miranda is not sure.

"I know I'll always be an alcoholic," she says slowly. "I mean, you can stay sober a long time, but if you start drinking again, you're going to get the exact same stuff happening in your life again. That's a given, you know? You won't suddenly be able to handle it, I guess. It just won't happen for you. Maybe if you're like a normal person, you can. But for me, and for other kids like me? Never. I should never drink.

Miranda says her life looks brighter now. "All I know is I learned about the consequences, and I'm glad I learned it now rather than, say, in my twenties or thirties."

"I can't say I will always go to AA meetings. I mean, I know some people do it their whole lives, but after a while it's the same thing, at least to me. And truthfully, I don't know if I'll ever drink again. I hope not, but who can tell? You can't make promises you can't keep. All I know is I learned about the consequences, and I'm glad I learned it now rather than, say, in my twenties or thirties."

Epilogue

In the time since these four young people were interviewed, a number of changes have occurred in their lives. His friends haven't heard from Joe, who six months ago was facing expulsion from a halfway house for chemically dependent teens. Attempts to reach him by telephone, or through agencies he was dealing with, have failed.

Miranda has run away. Her mother is shocked and disappointed that Miranda has disappeared. "I thought we were all done with this," she says sadly. "We have no idea where she is—maybe with a new boyfriend. I just wish she'd come home; I think she's in way over her head."

Ezra has left Sobriety High. He says that a situation occurred in which he and a number of others knew about a fellow student that was drinking. Even though they themselves were not drinking, they failed to turn in the student—a breach of school rules. He is in another sober school, which he says he enjoys. He plans on working a lot this summer, and earning money for a trip.

Melissa is busy and couldn't be happier. She is busy sponsoring several new teens at AA, and she herself remains sober. She is looking for a different part-time job and is enjoying college life.

Ways You Can Get Involved

THERE ARE MANY WAYS YOUNG
READERS CAN HELP THOSE WITH
ALCOHOLISM

Al-Anon and Al-Ateen Family Group Headquarters
1600 Corporate Landing Parkway
Virginia Beach, VA 23454
(800) 356-9996
Website: www.al-ateen.org

Al-Anon was formed to help the families of alcoholics; the Al-Ateen program is designed especially for teens who come from families with alcoholics. Both organizations hold local meetings throughout the country.

Alcoholics Anonymous
P.O. Box 459
Grand Central Station
New York, NY 10163
(212) 870-3400
Website: www.aa.org

AA believes that alcoholism is a disease, and that the only cure is total abstinence. They believe that members can solve their common problem and help one another through a twelve-step program that includes sharing experiences, hope, and strength.

Mothers Against Drunk Driving (MADD)
P.O. Box 541688
Dallas, TX 75345
(214) 744-6233

MADD is well-known for educating the public about the dangers of drunk driving. The organization encourages citizen participation in working towards reform of the drunk driving problem and the prevention of underage drinking acts. MADD acts as the voice of victims of drunk driving crashes by speaking in their behalf to schools, businesses, and community groups.

National Council on Alcoholism and Drug Dependence
12 W 21st St.
New York, NY 10010
(800) 622-2255
Website: www.ncadd.org

This group works for the prevention and treatment of alcoholism and other drug dependence through programs of public education, information, and public policy advocacy. NCADD sponsors National Alcohol Awareness Month each April.

For Further Reading

Alan R. Lang, *Alcohol: Teenage Drinking.* New York: Chelsea House, 1985. Excellent explanations of the physical effects of alcohol, especially on teenage nervous systems. Good historical background on alcoholism.

Ann Marie Pagliaro and Louis A. Pagliaro, *Substance Abuse Among Children and Adolescents.* New York: John Wiley and Sons, 1996. Although somewhat clinical in tone, this book gives invaluable data on treatment options, as well as expected rates of relapse for teens.

Herma Silverstein, *Alcoholism.* New York: Franklin Watts, 1990. Good section on treatment options, as well as a thorough look at what AA meetings are like.

Chris Varley, *Alcoholism.* New York: Marshall Cavendish, 1994. Very readable; informative section about the reasons people drink.

Index

About the Author

Gail B. Stewart is the author of more than eighty books for children and young adults. She lives in Minneapolis, Minnesota, with her husband, Carl, and their sons, Ted, Elliot, and Flynn. When she is not writing, she spends her time reading, walking, and watching her sons play soccer.

Although she has enjoyed working on each of her books, she says that *The Other America* series has been especially gratifying. "So many of my past books have involved extensive research," she says, "but most of it has been library work—journals, magazines, books. But for these books, the main research has been very human. Spending the day with a little girl who has AIDS, or having lunch in a soup kitchen with a homeless man—these kinds of things give you insight that a library alone just can't match."

Stewart hopes that readers of this series will experience some of the same insights—perhaps even being motivated to use some of the suggestions at the end of the each book to become involved with someone of the Other America.

About the Photographer

Carl Franzén is a writer/designer who enjoys using the camera to tell a story. He works out of his home in Minneapolis, where he lives with his wife, three boys, two dogs, and one cat. For lots of fun and camaraderie, he coaches a youth soccer team.